# STILL BECOMING

## A THERAPIST'S SACRED JOURNEY THROUGH DEPRESSION

DR. SWANZI SAUNDERS

LUCIDBOOKS

Still Becoming: A Therapist's Sacred Journey through Depression



Published by Lucid Books in Houston, TX
www.LucidBooks.com



ISBN: 978-1-63296-864-7
eISBN: 978-1-63296-865-4

Special Sales: Most Lucid Books titles are available in special quantity discounts. Custom imprinting or excerpting can also be done to fit special needs. Contact Lucid Books at Info@LucidBooks.com

With deep love and enduring gratitude, I dedicate this work to my husband, Carl; my three adult children, who now have children of their own; and my seven sisters. Your quiet faith steadied me, your love upheld me, and your encouragement breathed life into these pages.

# Contents

## PROLOGUE

# A Letter to the One Who's Still Becoming

*Dear Reader,*

*If you've picked up this book, something in you may be searching—perhaps for hope, or understanding, or simply the courage to keep going. You may be in a place of quiet struggle or slow healing. You may not have words for what you feel, or you may have far too many. Wherever you are, I want you to know: I get it. More importantly, God gets it—and He sees you.*

*This is not a book of easy answers. It is not a guide to quick fixes or a victorious story neatly tied up in a bow. It is a journey. A sacred one. And you are invited to walk it at your own pace.*

*I wrote these pages because I have walked through the valley of depression myself. I have felt the ache of being surrounded by love and still feeling lost. I have prayed in silence. I have questioned my faith. I have wondered if I would ever feel whole again. And I have learned—slowly and gently—that healing doesn't always come with fanfare. But it does come. Sometimes in pieces. Sometimes in stillness. And always in grace.*

*This book is about depression, yes, but it is also about faith, becoming, and the return of light. It's about discovering that healing is not just about feeling better. It's about being met, transformed, and restored. Not all at once. Not without questions. But deeply, and for good.*

*Wherever you are in your story, know that you are not alone. The path of healing may seem narrow and hidden, but it is not empty. Others have walked it. I have walked it. And I believe, with all my heart, that you will find light again.*

*So come as you are. Bring your questions, your weariness, your hope that barely flickers. There's no pressure here to be anything but real. You are already enough. You are already in motion.*

*You are still becoming.*

*With compassion and trust in the God who heals,*

*Dr. Swanzi*

CHAPTER 1

# A Personal Journey: Descending Through Darkness

I didn't see it coming. Depression crept in slowly, almost imperceptibly, until the weight of it was too much to ignore. What began as fatigue became a fog I couldn't lift, a sadness I couldn't name, a numbness that made even the simplest tasks feel impossible and unbearable. There was no clear trigger, no dramatic collapse. Just a slow descent into darkness.

This was years ago, before the rise of mental health awareness and therapy in my community and social circles. At the time, I was married with young children, a beautiful daughter and two handsome sons—three vibrant lives full of energy, wonder, and endless questions. They needed bedtime stories and after-school snacks, help with homework and hugs for reassurance. They needed me fully present. And from the outside, it looked like I was. I smiled when I needed to. I laughed at their jokes. I prayed with them at night. I cooked meals from scratch—lavish ones, even. But looking back, I can see now that I was trying to create meaning when I felt like I was disappearing. Cooking became my refuge, a place where my hands could keep moving even when my heart could not.

But inside? I was unraveling. Quietly. Invisibly. My thoughts ran rampant, and I was ashamed. *Why can't I just snap out of this? What is wrong with me? Does God even see this part of me—the version of me that's lost, silent, heavy, and scared?*

I was grateful for the life I had. I adored my family. I had faith. But beneath it all, I carried a question I didn't know how to answer: *How dare I feel such sadness when I have so much to be thankful for?* Was I ungrateful? Or worse—was I broken?

I wondered if this was what grief felt like. But grief over what? I hadn't lost anyone. And yet, I felt the weight of something gone. Something missing that I couldn't name. Was it me? Had I somehow disappeared beneath the responsibilities, the expectations, the effort to hold everything together?

I didn't have the language to name it as depression. I didn't know anyone who talked openly about mental health. There were no therapists in my circle. No doctor ever asked about my emotional state. Therapy, medication, even support groups—they weren't part of the world I knew. And so I walked this valley without professional help—not because I didn't need it, but because I didn't know it existed.

What I did have was a relationship with my Heavenly Father. And in those quiet, aching moments, I believed that if I could just pray hard enough, if I could somehow reach Him in the right way, He would lift this weight. That was my hope. That was my plea.

But most days, I couldn't find the words to pray. I opened my Bible and stared at the pages. I sat in silence, unsure if I was being faithful or failing. I whispered "Help" and hoped it was enough. I clung to Scripture, not because I felt inspired, but because I needed to believe that God still saw me—even in this version of myself that I didn't even recognize.

***There were no instant miracles.* Just a quiet presence and a gentle whisper: *You're not alone.***

There were countless moments of struggle. Days when I just couldn't get out of bed until the last possible minute. Nights when the darkness didn't just fall outside, it seeped into my spirit. There were hours lost to nothingness, when I sat staring without realizing it. But there were also fragments of grace.

My healing came in pieces. A sliver of energy here. A sudden moment of clarity there. A flicker of warmth during a prayer. A small laugh that surprised me. It wasn't dramatic or fast—but it was real.

One of the first signs of life returning was the desire to create. Not out of joy, but out of need. Making a meal from scratch reminded me I still had the capacity to make something. It grounded me. And when I folded tiny socks or packed lunches or held little hands in mine, I felt the faintest echo of love and purpose still alive in me, even when I couldn't feel it for myself.

I remember one night standing in the kitchen, dishes in the sink, the house finally quiet. And I cried—not out of despair, but out of exhaustion and longing. *What is this sadness? Why won't it leave?*

Looking back, I can see that depression was never the absence of faith. Instead, it was the battleground where my faith was being formed. Slowly, a deeper truth began to take shape—not the kind you shout from a mountaintop, but the kind you whisper in the valley: *God is still with me. I am still here.*

That truth didn't make the darkness disappear. But it gave me something to hold onto. A lifeline. A thread of grace that, somehow, never broke.

I've come to believe that my descent into depression was also an invitation—an invitation to a deeper kind of faith. Not one built on performance or perfect belief, but one rooted in presence. A faith that doesn't always have answers, but chooses to stay. A faith that says, *"Even here—even in this—I am being held."*

This journey didn't start with light. It started with loss. But it didn't end in darkness. And that is the story I want to tell—not one of tidy recovery, but of sacred unfolding. Of transformation that happened in the silence. Of grace that didn't always shout—but never let go.

## MOMENTS OF REFLECTION

- Have you ever experienced a season when you were showing up outwardly while struggling silently within? What was that like for you?

________________________________________

________________________________________

________________________________________

________________________________________

- What internal questions or self-judgments have surfaced for you in hard times?

  Can you identify thoughts like, *"Why can't I just snap out of this?" or "Does God even see this part of me?"*

________________________________________

________________________________________

________________________________________

________________________________________

- Have you ever felt the tension between gratitude and sadness—the feeling of being blessed but also broken? What emotions or memories rise up as you reflect on that?

________________________________________

________________________________________

________________________________________

- ❖ If you are in a season of heaviness now, what is one gentle truth you can hold onto today? What might it mean to trust that God sees even what feels invisible?

________________________________________

________________________________________

________________________________________

________________________________________

## CLOSING PRAYER

Dear God who sees in silence,
You met me when I didn't know how to pray.
You held me when I felt ashamed of my sadness.
You heard the questions I didn't dare speak out loud:
Why can't I shake this? Do You even see me here?
Thank You for staying when I thought I had to be stronger.
Thank You for whispering grace when I only had tears.
You never asked me to perform—only to be honest.
So here I am, Lord, honest and still becoming.
Hold me gently in the places I don't yet understand.
Give me courage to name what I feel,
And faith to believe that healing can begin
Even when I can't yet see the light.
In Jesus' name I pray. Amen.

**AFFIRMATION**

*I am allowed to feel broken and beloved at the same time. God sees what I cannot name. Even in the silence, I am being held. And my healing has already begun.*

# CHAPTER 2

# I'm Not Alone: A National Perspective

In my deepest struggle with depression, I felt completely alone. I thought no one else could possibly understand the emptiness I felt. I didn't know that what I was going through had a name. I didn't know that millions of others were quietly fighting the same battle.

There's something powerful in realizing we're not alone—not only spiritually, but socially. Depression is not rare, and it is not a sign of weakness. It is a shared human experience, affecting people from every walk of life. Recognizing that truth is not only comforting, it's freeing.

### *Depression is a quiet epidemic of the soul.*

Depression isn't confined to a few—it quietly affects countless lives. For example, data sources report major depression as one of the most common mental disorders, impacting an estimated 21 million people in the United States. The demographics are across the board, affecting both males and females, people of all ages, races and ethnicities, and those with varying socio-economic backgrounds. It slips into homes, churches, workplaces, and families, often without being seen or named. It wears different faces—fatigue, irritability, numbness, isolation. And it rarely announces itself. Many who suffer do so behind a smile, behind service, behind faith. And because it's so often misunderstood or hidden, it becomes not only a personal battle, but a deeply isolating one.

Understanding that depression is widespread, and deeply human, can shift the way we see ourselves and others. It helps remove shame. It breaks the silence. It invites us to extend grace.

### *Depression wears many faces.*

When we think of depression, we often think of sadness. And while sadness can be a hallmark symptom, it's not the whole picture. In fact, not everyone with depression feels sadness in the way others might expect. Some people never cry. Some don't even feel particularly "down." And yet, they are suffering. Quietly. Profoundly. Deeply.

For many, depression is a sense of emotional numbness or disconnection. It presents itself as an inability to feel joy, known as *anhedonia.* In other words, things that once brought life now feel flat. Laughter becomes forced. Relationships feel distant. Nothing seems worth the effort.

Others experience depression primarily in their bodies—through exhaustion, disrupted sleep, unexplained aches and pains, or a constant feeling of heaviness. These physical symptoms often mask the deeper emotional pain, making it harder to recognize what's really happening.

Some feel it as irritability, frustration, or anger. It could show up in short tempers, mood swings, or a deep sense of being overwhelmed. For men and children especially, depression can present more as agitation than sadness.

Still others experience cognitive symptoms: a fog that dulls concentration, impairs memory, or makes decisions feel impossible. Or they may wrestle with silent thoughts of worthlessness and guilt—feelings that aren't tied to any specific event, yet still oppressive.

Depression can also take the form of social withdrawal. Not because people don't care, but because connection takes energy they no longer have. They may isolate not to be dramatic, but because the noise of the world is too much. Or they may simply feel unworthy of love and support.

And often, there is a deep hopelessness—a quiet despair that whispers, *"What's the point?"* It's not always dramatic. It's not always visible. But it's real.

For some, that despair deepens into thoughts of ending their life. Suicidal ideation—though not experienced by everyone—is a very real symptom of clinical depression. It may begin as a passive wish to disappear or escape pain, but it can progress into more serious, active thoughts of suicide. These thoughts are not attention-seeking or selfish. They are signals of immense suffering and should never be ignored. Suicidal ideation requires compassionate attention, open conversation, and professional support. If you or someone you love is experiencing these thoughts, know this: *there is help. There is hope. And you are not alone.*

The truth is, depression wears many faces. It is more than sadness. And when we broaden our understanding of how it manifests, we make more room for compassion—both for ourselves and for others.

### *There is no shame in struggling.*

Let this be said plainly: there is no shame in depression. No shame in needing help. No shame in reaching out for support—spiritual, emotional, or medical. In fact, it's an act of strength and wisdom to do so.

In spiritual communities, depression is sometimes misunderstood. People may be told to "pray more" or to "have more faith," as if depression is a purely spiritual failure. But depression is not a lack of faith. It's an illness, a wound of the soul and the body.

The truth is faithful people can suffer deeply. Prophets, saints, and modern believers alike have walked through seasons of anguish. King David cried out in Psalm 13:1, *"O Lord, how long will you forget me? Forever? How long will you look the other way?"* Even Jesus, in His humanity, wept and groaned under the weight of sorrow.

You are in good company. And more importantly, you

are not forgotten. If you are struggling, know that you're part of a vast and resilient community. And healing begins when we speak the truth: I'm not okay. But I want to be.

***Special Note: When the struggle feels too dark or heavy, there is help and hope.**

> *If you are struggling with thoughts of ending your life, please know this: you are not alone, and you are not beyond help. Depression can cloud your vision, but God sees you clearly—and lovingly. There is no shame in seeking support. You were not meant to carry this pain alone.*
>
> *In the United States, you can call or text the 988 Suicide & Crisis Lifeline at any time, day or night. Simply dial 988 or visit 988lifeline.org. Trained counselors are ready to listen and help, without judgment.*
>
> *Outside the U.S., please reach out to a local crisis line, hospital, or mental health provider. For a directory of international suicide prevention resources, visit befrienders.org or search for mental health services available in your region.*
>
> *Whether you speak with a counselor, a pastor, a doctor, or a trusted friend—reaching out is an act of courage, not weakness. Your life matters. Your story is not over. And even now, in this very moment, God is near.*

## MOMENTS OF REFLECTION

- Have you ever believed you were alone in your suffering? What challenged or reinforced that belief?

- Which less-recognized symptoms of depression have you experienced or seen in others?

- How can understanding the many faces of depression shift the way you respond to your own pain or someone else's?

❖ What would it look like to replace shame with self-compassion?

________________________________________

________________________________________

________________________________________

________________________________________

## CLOSING PRAYER

Dear God of the multitude and the one,
Thank You for reminding me that I'm not alone –
not in my sorrow, not in my silence, not in my struggle.
Help me to release the shame I've carried
and to embrace the truth of my humanity.
Let me see myself and others with compassion.
And when I forget how many others have walked this road,
remind me that healing is never a solitary path –
it is a shared journey.
In Jesus' name I pray. Amen.

### AFFIRMATION

*I am not alone. Depression wears many faces, but God sees mine. There is no shame in what I carry. Healing begins with compassion—for myself and for others.*

CHAPTER 3

# The Whole-Person Affect: The Brain—And Beyond

When I was walking through depression, I often wondered, *What's wrong with me?* I couldn't pinpoint a single cause. There were emotional wounds, spiritual exhaustion, physical fatigue, and mental fog. It felt like every part of me—body, mind, and spirit—was unraveling.

It wasn't until much later that I began to understand that depression doesn't affect just one part of us. It impacts the whole person. And real healing requires us to tend to every layer of who we are. We are beautifully complex. And so is our suffering.

### *The body bears the weight of the soul.*

Depression doesn't live only in the mind. It often settles into the body, quietly and insistently. We may feel it as fatigue that no amount of sleep can fix, or as a heaviness in our chest, limbs, or gut. It might show up in chronic pain, frequent illness, or sudden changes in appetite and sleep. The body begins to speak when the soul is burdened beyond what it can carry silently.

I didn't realize at the time that my physical weariness was connected to my emotional pain. But looking back, I see it clearly: my body was absorbing the ache I hadn't yet named. And in its own way, it was crying out for attention and compassion.

This isn't weakness. It's wisdom: the wisdom of the body. Our bodies hold stories long before we have the words to tell them. They remember stress, carry the residue of trauma, and sometimes mirror emotions we've pushed aside. When we don't know how to grieve, the body grieves for us. When we're not yet able to cry, the body tightens, aches, or shuts down. The body is both messenger and participant in our healing.

There were days when I couldn't explain why I was so tired, why my muscles ached, or why I felt heavy even in moments of quiet. But my body knew. It was bearing the emotional weight that I couldn't articulate yet. It was trying to get my attention—not to scare me, but to invite me into deeper care.

When I began to treat my body not as something to push through, but as something to listen to, a subtle shift occurred. I started noticing the early signs of burnout or sadness in physical form—a clenched jaw, a racing heart, and a lack of appetite. And rather than ignore those signals, I began to respond. I started to ask, *"What is my body trying to tell me?"* And in doing so, I began to offer compassion to the parts of me I had long ignored.

Our bodies are not separate from our inner world. They are the vessels that carry our stories, our burdens, and our hopes. Honoring the wisdom of our bodies is one of the first steps toward healing the whole self.

### *Thoughts and feelings can turn against us.*

Depression can distort our thoughts and hijack our emotions. It turns ordinary struggles into overwhelming narratives. It tries to convince us that we are hopeless, unworthy, or irreparably broken. Our inner dialogue becomes a loop of criticism and despair, often fueled by shame or past wounds. Over time, we start to believe these inner messages are true.

Emotionally, we may swing between numbness and sadness, irritability and deep shame. Sometimes we cry without knowing why. Other times we feel flat, like life has lost its color and meaning. It's easy to mistake these symptoms for personal flaws rather than signs of an illness that affects both mind and mood.

One of the greatest gifts therapy offers, particularly approaches like Cognitive Behavioral Therapy (CBT), is a way to observe and untangle these patterns. We learn to notice our thoughts without being consumed by them. We begin to question the distorted thinking and lies, and we start to practice responding to ourselves with truth and grace. And over time, our thoughts become allies again. Our emotions soften. And we remember: *We are not our depression.* We are still here, still held, and still deeply loved.

### ***Sometimes, there's a longing too deep for words.***

There is a kind of longing that can't be spoken. It's a soul-deep ache not easily explained or soothed. For many walking through depression, this longing is spiritual. And it's not always dramatic. Often, it's a quiet yearning for God's nearness, a desire to feel seen, heard, and held again. And yet, in the very moment when we most long for divine comfort, God can feel painfully far away.

I remember sitting in silence, Bible open, heart heavy, longing for something—and feeling nothing. My prayers felt hollow, like words floating into space. I still believed God was real, but I didn't feel Him. I questioned whether He heard me, whether He cared, whether I was doing something wrong, whether I had somehow lost His presence for good.

This is one of the cruelest tensions of spiritual depression: our spirit longs for God even as our mind doubts, our emotions go numb, and our faith feels threadbare. It is the ache of reaching for something you can no longer feel, the heartbreak of praying into silence and wondering if heaven has closed its ears. Deep down, you remember the nearness of God. You remember what it felt like to worship freely, to believe confidently, to feel moved by Scripture or song. But now? That memory feels like someone else's story.

Your spirit still whispers, *"I want to believe,"* but your thoughts quickly follow with, *"What if none of this helps?"* You open your Bible hoping for comfort but find only disconnection. You bow your head to pray, but the words feel empty or forced. A strange kind of grief rises—not just over your emotional pain, but over the seeming loss of intimacy with God. And yet—even in this tug-of-war between longing and disbelief, something holy remains: the longing itself.

***To long for God in the silence is still faith.***

To crave comfort in the numbness is still evidence of connection. Your doubts do not disqualify you from grace. They are part of the wrestling. And God, who met Jacob in the night and Thomas in his questioning, does not withdraw from those who struggle. He draws closer.

Sometimes, the deepest faith is not found in certainty. It's found in continuing to reach for God when everything in you feels unsure. This tension, as painful as it is, becomes the soil where honest faith can take root.

There's no shame in feeling disconnected from God. The Psalms are filled with cries of longing and confusion. Consider the yearning in Psalm 10:1: *"O Lord, why do you stand so far away? Why do you hide when I am in trouble?"* or *"I thirst for God, the living God. When can I go and stand before him?"* in Psalm 42:2. Even Jesus, in His darkest hour, cried out, *"My God, my God, why have you abandoned me?"* (Matthew 27:46)

These aren't words of weak faith. They are words of *honest* faith. Of souls that continue to reach for God even when the light is dim. Of spirits longing to be met, even when they no longer know how to pray.

The truth is this: *God's silence is not absence.* His stillness is not neglect. Even when we feel nothing, He is still near. He dwells not just in celebration, but in suffering. Not only in clarity, but in mystery. Sometimes, He speaks most powerfully in what we experience as silence. This can be hard to believe when our prayers seem to echo back to us unanswered, or when worship feels mechanical instead of meaningful. But Scripture reminds us again and again: God is not only the God of thunder and miracles—He is also the God of whispers, of waiting, of wilderness. He does not vanish when we can no longer feel His presence. Instead, He becomes the quiet strength that sustains us when emotion fails.

Sometimes, what feels like divine silence is actually sacred stillness—a stillness that invites us to lean in, to listen differently, to trust more deeply. Like seeds planted in the earth, transformation often happens beneath the surface, in places we cannot yet see. God's presence doesn't always announce itself with immediacy. Sometimes it arrives with the soft persistence of breath, with the grace to make it through another day, with the flicker of hope that refuses to die.

If you feel nothing, it does not mean God has gone. If you hear nothing, it does not mean He has stopped speaking. In fact, some of the most profound encounters with God begin in these very places—when everything else is stripped away. We learn to recognize His nearness not by what we feel, but by what we know to be true. Hold on. God is not absent. He is attending to you even now—with quiet care, with faithful love, and with a presence more constant than your pain.

### *Hold on to what you know in the dark.*

When you cannot feel God, hold on to what you've already seen of Him. Remember how He carried you before, even when you didn't realize it at the time. Recall the moments when peace came unexpectedly, or when His Word stirred something deep within you. Let those memories be like stones of remembrance—anchors in the fog.

When prayer feels empty, remember that the Spirit intercedes for you with groans too deep for words. Consider the words of Romans 8:26: *"And the Holy Spirit helps us in our weakness. For example, we don't know what God wants us to pray for. But the Holy Spirit prays for us with groanings that cannot be expressed in words."* You are not praying alone. Heaven is speaking on your behalf, even when your mouth cannot form a single sentence. You don't have to impress God with your prayers. You don't have to explain yourself. He already knows your heart. He knows the sorrow you haven't named, the ache behind your silence, the questions behind your eyes. He sees it all, and still, He draws near.

This longing you feel? It's not weakness. It's sacred ground. It may feel like neediness, or like failure, but it is something much more profound—it is the soul's cry for connection with its Creator. It is the echo of Eden within you, the part of your spirit that remembers what it means to walk with God in the cool of the day.

This ache, this yearning for something more, is not a sign that you've lost your way. It's a sign that God is still calling you deeper.

Longing is a form of faith. It says, "Even if I don't feel You, I still want You." And that desire, even in its raw and painful form, is itself a gift. It is part of how God is drawing you back to Himself—not through force or fear, but through longing, through love. So hold on. Not to your feelings, but to what you know of God's character. He is still good. He is still present. And even now, even here, He is still drawing near.

### *Depression is rarely the result of one cause—more often, it's a convergence of many.*

For some, depression begins with a quiet shift in brain chemistry, a family history that quietly lays the groundwork. For others, it is triggered by seasons of profound stress, chronic illness, or hormonal changes that send ripples through the body's internal balance. There are those whose depression is rooted in wounds from the past—unresolved trauma, rejection, or loss that was never given the space to heal. And there are others still who suffer under the weight of environmental burdens: poverty, racism, chronic caregiving, isolation, or the persistent pressure to perform in a world that rarely stops to notice suffering.

These influential factors are important to name—not to place blame or to create a list of problems to fix, but to acknowledge the full picture of what we carry.

- Neurological predispositions (e.g., family history, brain chemistry)
- Physiological stressors (e.g., chronic illness, hormonal shifts, fatigue)
- Psychological wounds (e.g., trauma, abuse, complicated grief)
- Environmental pressures (e.g., poverty, loneliness, overstimulation, or disconnection)

When we consider these contributors, we begin to understand depression not as a moral failing or a spiritual deficiency, but as a deeply human condition, one that arises in the body, manifests in the mind, and often weaves its way into our spirit and sense of meaning.

Recognizing this complexity does not make healing harder. It makes it more human. It reminds us that our suffering is not imagined, and it invites us to hold our healing with reverence and care. It teaches us that our thoughts are not the whole story. That our bodies deserve gentleness. That our souls, weary as they may be, are still longing for light. To know this is to begin to extend compassion toward ourselves.

You are not broken beyond repair. You are layered, and your healing will be layered too.

Approach yourself tenderly—because every part of you, from the chemistry of your brain to the ache in your spirit, is worthy of healing. This is not about fixing yourself. It is about honoring the fullness of who you are and allowing God's grace to reach every layer.

### *Choose to become whole, one gentle step at a time.*

Healing rarely comes with fanfare. It doesn't always look like progress. More often, it unfolds quietly—through slow mornings, small acts of courage, and sacred pauses. Depression has a way of fragmenting us, pulling the body in one direction, the mind in another, and leaving the spirit feeling abandoned somewhere in between. But healing—true healing—invites us back into unity. It calls us home to ourselves.

It's not an overnight process. It's not about arriving quickly or "fixing" what's broken. It's about learning to listen again to the wisdom of your body, to the voice of your thoughts, to the ache of your spirit. It's about offering yourself the same compassion you would freely give to others.

Wholeness is not about perfection. It's about presence. It's not about having all the answers. It's about alignment—living from a place where your body, mind, and spirit can move in the same direction again, even if slowly. Wholeness begins when we stop asking, *"What's wrong with me?"* and start asking, *"What part of me is longing to be heard, held, or healed?"*

You may begin with the physical, allowing yourself to rest, to move gently, to eat when you're hungry and sleep when you're tired. Or you may begin with your thoughts, gently questioning the narratives you've absorbed, speaking truth to the deceptions that have taken root. Or perhaps it starts in the silence, simply making space for your soul to breathe without expectation or pressure. Each of these is a step toward wholeness.

Every small act of care becomes a sacred defiance against despair. Every moment you choose to stay—stay present, stay kind, stay hopeful—is a quiet declaration: *I am still becoming. And I am worth the becoming.*

You don't need to know the whole path. You don't need to be fearless. You only need to begin. The invitation isn't to strive. It's to choose. Choose gentleness over judgment. Choose presence over pressure. Choose to believe that God, who formed every intricate part of you, is already at work in places you cannot yet see. Choose to believe that healing is not a race, but a sacred unfolding.

You are not just recovering. You are being restored. Reclaimed. Remade.

And you are not doing it alone.

God is walking with you through every layer—body, mind, and spirit—bringing all things into healing. Not in haste, but in holiness. Not through striving, but through grace. Not once and for all, but day by day. You are still becoming.

## MOMENTS OF REFLECTION

- Which part of your being—body, mind, or spirit—feels most in need of care and compassion today? What is it asking from you—rest, truth, connection, grace?

  ______________________________

  ______________________________

  ______________________________

  ______________________________

- Where might your body be speaking wisdom that your mind has struggled to hear?

  ______________________________

  ______________________________

  ______________________________

  ______________________________

- In what ways have you felt spiritually disconnected in the past? What helped, even in a small way, to draw you back to a sense of connection?

  ______________________________

  ______________________________

  ______________________________

  ______________________________

❖ What would it mean for you to welcome healing as a layered process rather than a single solution?

______________________________________________

______________________________________________

______________________________________________

______________________________________________

## CLOSING PRAYER

Dear God of every layer,
You formed me—body, mind, and spirit—with amazing intention.
You know my depths, my silence, my scattered pieces.
When I feel fragmented, draw me back to wholeness.
When I try to numb my pain, teach me to listen again.
When I rush toward answers, slow me down to notice You.
Thank You for the wisdom You've woven into my body,
for the truth that renews my mind,
and for the grace that heals my spirit.
I surrender to the step-by-step work You are doing in me.
Help me not to despise the small steps.
Help me to trust the healing I cannot yet see.
And when I feel undone, remind me:
You are still making me whole.
In Jesus' name I pray. Amen.

**AFFIRMATION**

*I am fearfully and wonderfully made—body, mind, and spirit. My healing is unfolding with gentleness and grace. I choose wholeness—not perfection, but presence. God is restoring every part of me. I am still becoming.*

# CHAPTER 4

# What We Can't See: An Exploration of Spiritual Causes

For a long time, I believed my depression was purely emotional. Then I began to wonder if it was physical. Later still, I saw how much it affected my thoughts. But something deeper kept rising to the surface, something I couldn't fully explain.

It was a *spiritual ache—a* sense of disconnection, disorientation, even oppression. Though I had faith, I felt spiritually numb. Though I prayed, I often felt unheard. Though I knew God was real, I struggled to feel His nearness. I came to understand something: while depression often has biological and psychological roots, it can also have a spiritual dimension, one that is just as real, just as painful, and just as in need of healing.

***Sometimes, there's an ache beneath the science.***

It is true—depression can be influenced by brain chemistry, trauma, stress, or genetics. These are real, tangible factors. And recognizing them has brought enormous breakthroughs in mental health care. However, to reduce depression to biology *only* is like trying to describe the ocean by measuring its salt content. There's more beneath the surface. Much more.

Depression, for many, carries undercurrents that defy easy explanation. Beneath the fatigue and fog, beneath the symptoms and diagnoses, there is often a spiritual ache—a longing that no scan can reveal, no data can measure. These are the parts of the experience that live in the soul.

It's like standing before a stained-glass window in the dark. All the pieces are there—shaped, fitted, and beautiful in their own right. But unless the light shines through, the pattern remains hidden. The structure exists, but the deeper meaning is obscured. Likewise, when we approach depression only through the lens of science, we may understand its structure, but we miss the whole story. We miss the soul's silent cries for connection, the soul's search for meaning, the soul's longing for God.

For me, that spiritual ache felt more like disorientation than despair. Yes, I still believed in God, but I questioned His nearness. I tried to pray, but the words came out hollow. I opened Scripture and just felt numb. The ache wasn't loud—it was haunting. It whispered questions I didn't know how to answer: *Why can't I feel Him? Is He hiding? Or have I wandered too far?*

Even as I understood that depression involved my body and mind, I also sensed that there was something at work on a deeper level. I wasn't just tired. I wasn't just emotionally drained. I was spiritually homesick. I hadn't lost my faith, but I couldn't feel the nearness of the God I loved. It was as if I had been exiled from the comfort of His presence, unable to find my way back. I missed the warmth of connection, the ease of prayer, the sense that He was walking beside me. And though I still believed in Him, I longed to feel Him again—not just in my mind, but in the depths of my soul. That's the part science can't fully account for—the ache beneath the symptoms, the longing beneath the logic. That longing is real. And in many cases, it is spiritual.

This is not to diminish the value of psychological insight or medical support. On the contrary, those tools are crucial. But as people of faith, people of spirit, we must also be willing to explore the deeper layers. To ask not only *What is happening in my body?* but also *What is happening in my soul?*

The presence of a spiritual dimension doesn't mean we've failed in our faith. It simply means we're human. It means that our hearts, minds, and spirits are deeply interconnected, and that suffering can touch every part of us, even the places we once felt most secure. To feel spiritually disoriented or distant from God during depression is not a sign of spiritual weakness. It's a sign that we are whole beings, carrying wounds in places both visible and invisible. And just as our pain can be multi-layered—emotional, physical, mental, and spiritual—so too must our healing be layered. We may need prayer *and* rest. Scripture *and* support. Faith *and* therapy. There is no contradiction in that. There is only grace meeting us at every level of our need.

***Sometimes, the battle is indeed spiritual.***

Sometimes, what we experience in depression feels more than emotional or cognitive—it feels spiritual. Not just a chemical imbalance or a cognitive distortion, but something heavier, more accusing. It may come in the form of persistent shame, an overwhelming sense of unworthiness, or a deep conviction that God has turned away. At times, it may feel as though despair isn't just rising from within your own thoughts—it's pressing in from outside, like a force whispering lies into your spirit: that you're too broken, too far gone, or utterly alone. These moments are not mere emotional lows; they can feel like spiritual assaults, attacks on your identity, your belonging, your very sense of hope.

Recognizing this dynamic is not about blaming everything on the enemy, but about honoring the truth that healing requires discernment. Some of the voices we hear in our pain are not our own. They echo lies we've absorbed or battles we were never meant to fight. And some of the burdens we carry were never ours to begin with. That's why it's important to consider the possibility of spiritual oppression—not as the sole cause, but as a meaningful layer that may be influencing the depth and persistence of our pain.

In these moments, it may not just be a matter of negative thinking or imbalance. It may actually be spiritual warfare, what Scripture refers to as oppression. Paul writes in Ephesians 6:12, "For we are not flighting against flesh-and-blood enemies, but against evil rulers and authorities of the unseen world, against mighty powers in this dark world, and against evil spirits in the heavenly places." This kind of spiritual conflict doesn't always manifest in dramatic ways.

Sometimes, it's subtle and persistent, a constant inner voice whispering, *You're worthless. You'll never be free. God is done with you.* These voices aren't merely discouraging. They are accusing. Condemning. They don't lead to repentance or conviction—they lead to hopelessness and shame. And they contradict everything God says about who we are in Christ.

When we ignore the possibility of spiritual oppression, we may find ourselves fighting a battle with only part of the armor God has provided. But when we begin to discern it, we can bring it into the light. We can name the lies and speak truth. We can cry out to the God who still delivers. We can stand in the authority of Christ, who came to heal the brokenhearted and to set the captives free.

Spiritual oppression doesn't mean you're spiritually weak. In fact, it's often a sign that something in you is still reaching for light—still resisting the pull of despair. And that resistance is not your own strength—it's His grace alive in you, even when you can't feel it.

The good news is this: darkness does not get the final word. "The light shines in the darkness, and the darkness can never extinguish it" (John 1:5). And that light still shines, even in the most shadowed places of your soul.

### ***Sometimes, there's unresolved grief, guilt, and purpose.***

Not all spiritual burdens come from external forces. Some live quietly within us as unresolved grief, lingering guilt, or a deep loss of meaning. These burdens don't always manifest as a crisis. Oftentimes, they settle in as a quiet ache, a low, persistent sorrow that we learn to live with, even as it drains our energy and distorts our sense of connection to God, others, and ourselves.

Sometimes, we carry grief we've never given ourselves permission to feel. Perhaps we've minimized a loss or pushed it aside in the name of strength or survival. Other times, we hold guilt for things we've already confessed, you know, guilt for things that God has forgiven even though we haven't yet released them. And then there's the ache of a kind of disorientation, a haunting sense that our life has drifted from meaning, that we're no longer sure what we're here for, who we've become or are becoming. These aren't signs of spiritual failure. They are signs of being human.

God never asked us to carry these things alone. In fact, healing often begins with something as simple as *naming what we carry*. Not to fix it in a moment, but to acknowledge its presence in the presence of a God who is not afraid of our sorrow and shame, and understands and even welcomes our questions. This kind of spiritual healing doesn't always arrive in flashes of insight or immediate freedom. It may come through counseling and community, through lament and confession, through tears in prayer or sacred silence. Sometimes, it comes not through answers, but through *companionship with God in the mystery.* What matters most is the posture of the heart: a willingness to come honestly, and a trust that God will meet us there—with tenderness, not condemnation.

### *Consider a sacred shift in your healing*

What if healing isn't about returning to who you once were? What if it's about becoming someone new—someone more rooted, more whole, more deeply attuned to the voice of God? So often, we view healing as a return. A going back. We long for the peace we once felt, the clarity we once had, the energy we used to rely on. But true spiritual healing rarely works that way. It's not about returning—it's about *becoming*. And becoming takes time. This is the sacred shift.

The sacred shift is the movement from grasping for relief to surrendering into transformation. From pleading for escape to trusting the oftentimes slow work of renewal. It's a shift that invites us to stop measuring progress only by how much we've overcome, and instead ask: *"How much have I surrendered? How much more am I willing to be shaped?"*

When we make this shift, healing stops being something we wait for and becomes something we partner with God to cultivate. It happens not just in mountaintop moments, but in daily trust. In small choices. In quiet prayers. In long exhalations where we release our timelines and welcome grace.

God is not primarily concerned with symptom management. He's after soul restoration. And that kind of restoration touches everything: our past wounds, our present doubts, and our future purpose. He goes to the places we've buried, the deceptions we've believed, and the pain we've tried to silence. He doesn't barge in with demands. Rather, He enters gently, like light finding its way through a cracked door. He works slowly, not because He is distant, but because He is intentional. He's not trying to rush us. He's trying to remake us.

### *Healing is not a bypass—it's an invitation*

Spiritual healing is not about bypassing your emotions. It doesn't ask you to ignore your psychological needs or override your physical ones. Remember, it's an invitation to wholeness, a call to let God tend to every layer of your being. It's the integration of spirit, mind, and body under the care of a loving Creator who sees all, knows all, and still loves us all. This kind of healing is not passive. It's lived into. One moment at a time. One prayer at a time. One choice to trust, rest, or speak honestly at a time. You don't have to strive for it. You simply have to say yes to it.

God is already at work. He's been drawing you closer not in spite of your brokenness, but through it. He's not waiting at the finish line. He's walking beside you, healing what you can't yet see and whispering truth when deceptions grow loud.

Let this be your sacred shift: from resistance to receptivity. From shame to self-compassion. From surviving to being *remade*. You are not too far gone. You are not behind. You are not disqualified. You are in the process of becoming whole.

## MOMENTS OF REFLECTION

❖ What spiritual burdens—such as grief, guilt, or disconnection—might you be carrying quietly beneath the surface?

________________________________________

________________________________________

________________________________________

________________________________________

❖ Are there areas of your life where you have been asking for relief, but sensing an invitation to deeper renewal? If so, what are they?

________________________________________

________________________________________

________________________________________

________________________________________

❖ Have you experienced moments of a sacred shift, where healing felt less like a solution and more like transformation?

______________________________________

______________________________________

______________________________________

______________________________________

❖ How might God be inviting you to surrender—not just your pain, but your expectations of what healing "should" look like?

______________________________________

______________________________________

______________________________________

______________________________________

## CLOSING PRAYER

Dear God of the deep and hidden places,
You see what no one else sees.
You know the burdens I carry –
the grief I've buried, the guilt I've held, the ache I can't explain.
You know how I've longed for relief, and how afraid I am to be fully seen.

Yet You do not turn away.
You come close. You speak gently.
You offer not just healing, but transformation.
Teach me to stop striving to return to who I once was.
Show me how to surrender to the sacred shift,
To trust that You are not rushing me, but remaking me.
When I resist, remind me that You are patient.
When I forget, remind me that You are near.
Let me lean into this journey, layer by layer,
not for perfection, but for wholeness.
And let Your love be the truth I rest in, now and always.
In Jesus' name I pray. Amen.

### AFFIRMATION

*I am not beyond healing. I am not who I once was, and I do not need to be. God is gently remaking me, layer by layer, breath by breath, in truth, in grace, and in His love. This is my sacred shift. And I am becoming whole.*

## CHAPTER 5

# Found: A Light in the Darkness

There comes a moment in many healing journeys when we realize that a shift has taken place indeed—not always dramatically, not even clearly. But it's enough to notice. There comes the realization: the darkness is not total. There's a glimmer of light.

For me, that moment didn't come with trumpets. And yes, there were still those moments of tears. The shift came softly, though. Quietly. Through a sense of stillness in prayer, a bit of energy returning to my body, a flicker of interest in something I'd once enjoyed and had lost interest in. I couldn't say I was "well," but I could say I was no longer completely lost. Somehow, amidst the dark, I had an undeniable sense of being found.

***Prayer became the beginning of my return.***

For me, prayer was not a dramatic rescue, but a quiet, persistent lifeline. In the thick of depression, my prayers were not eloquent, to say the least. As a matter of fact, they were often wordless—just a sigh, a groan, or the soft whisper of *"Help me."* That was all I could manage. But those quiet, unformed cries were enough. They were sacred in their simplicity—raw, unrehearsed, honest, authentic. They didn't need to be impressive—or theologically sound, for that matter. They only needed to be real.

Over time, I came to see that prayer didn't require my strength—just my presence. I didn't have to climb my way to God. I just had to show up, even if I had nothing to offer but silence and tears. And in that silent offering, something began to shift.

Gradually, my spirit began to respond. Not because I forced it. Not because I tried to manufacture faith or feeling. But because prayer, even in its most fragile form, became an anchor—a steady place in the storm. It reminded me, gently and quietly, that I was not alone. That God heard me, even when my voice cracked and trembled. That He saw me, even when I couldn't see Him. That He remained near, even when my heart felt numb.

Let me be clear about this: prayer did *not* erase my depression. It didn't wave a wand over my pain and make it disappear. But it did something much deeper. It created space for hope to return. And hope—even a flicker—is light. It doesn't have to be bright to be real. It just has to be present.

There were no fireworks. No breakthrough moments. Just a slow unfolding. Just the quiet miracle of being held when I couldn't hold myself. And in that holding, I was slowly being found.

### *Trust often grows in the dark.*

I learned that trust doesn't always arrive in bright light. Sometimes, it's born in silence. In uncertainty. In the long nights when answers don't come and the future is clouded with questions. We often think of trust as something strong and confident. But in my experience, it often begins as something fragile—something we whisper rather than declare.

During my darkest days, I wanted assurance. I wanted God to show me the outcome, to make me feel better, to promise that healing would come quickly. But that's not how trust was formed in me. It didn't come through clear answers. It came through quiet surrender. I began to trust not because I felt sure, but because I chose to believe I was still being held.

At first, my trust was simply staying present in prayer, even when I felt nothing. It was breathing through the uncertainty instead of fighting it. It was doing the next right thing when I had no idea what came after that. And slowly, that kind of trust became my anchor.

I learned that God does some of His deepest work not in clarity, but in mystery. Not in control, but in surrender. And I learned that the dark isn't always the absence of God—it's often the soil where trust takes root.

Trust, I've come to understand, is a lot like the moonflower. It doesn't bloom in the brightness of certainty, but in the hush of night. It opens quietly, in stillness, when the world is watching something else. You don't force a moonflower open; you wait, you watch, and eventually, it begins to unfold—petal by petal, breath by breath—without spectacle, but with grace.

Or perhaps trust is like the ghost pipe—that pale, otherworldly blossom that doesn't draw strength from sunlight like most plants, but from a hidden underground network of roots and mycelium. It draws its sustenance from places unseen. Its very survival depends on connections it cannot see, only sense.

There are certain kinds of growth—beautiful, lasting, and deep—that only happen in the dark. We don't see the roots as they deepen. We don't hear the quiet hum of restoration beneath the surface. But in the shadows, transformation is still happening. Healing is still taking root.

Trust doesn't always come with clarity. Sometimes it arrives without answers. It develops slowly—like dew on morning grass—almost imperceptible until the light hits it just right. It is the kind of growth that whispers rather than shouts, the kind that takes shape not when everything is resolved, but when we learn to stay, to rest, and to believe in what we cannot yet see.

And perhaps that's where faith is most alive—not in the absence of doubt, but in the choice to reach toward something holy and unseen, even while still trembling.

If you're in that place now, where the path is unclear, and the light feels dim, know this: You are not doing it wrong. You are not lost. You are growing something worthwhile. One quiet choice at a time, trust is being formed in you. And one day, you'll look back and realize that what you planted in the dark has begun to bloom in the light.

One of the richest lessons I learned was how to trust God in the middle of the journey, not just when things got better, but when I still felt unsure, incomplete, unfinished. This kind of trust didn't come from certainty. It came from surrender. I stopped trying to fix myself. I stopped striving to "get it right." I simply let myself be held. I chose to believe that God was guiding me, even if I couldn't feel the direction. That was the kind of trust that became a turning point for me. It was quiet, but it was real. It diffused my anxiety. It deepened my faith. It became the light on my path forward as hope quietly returned.

### *With hope came discernment in the darkness.*

As hope gently returned, so did something else: *discernment.* Not the kind that shouts instructions or lights up the whole path, but a soft knowing. A subtle sense of when to speak and when to be still. A growing awareness of what was drawing me closer to peace—and what was pulling me further from it.

At first, I didn't recognize it as discernment. Instead of flashing signs or bold declarations, I became aware of a subtle tuning of the soul. It felt like a gentle pull toward what was life-giving: quiet stillness, Scripture, music, nature, and quiet connection with trusted people. These weren't dramatic revelations. They were soft invitations, whispers of grace, that gradually helped me notice what my soul needed in order to heal.

Quiet stillness helped me hear again. Not with my ears, but with my spirit. In the stillness, I could sense what brought peace and what disturbed it. It became a place where I could breathe, feel, and begin to sort through the noise.

Scripture offered gentle orientation—not rigid answers, but sacred echoes of truth that grounded me when everything else felt unstable. Certain verses seemed to shimmer when I read them, not because they fixed anything, but because they reminded me that I was not alone, not forgotten.

Music helped me feel when I was too numb for words. Certain lyrics and melodies became prayers of their own—bridges between Heaven and my aching heart. I discovered that discernment often rises not through logic, but through resonance—when something true within us responds to something greater outside of us.

Nature became a gentle teacher in my healing. It reminded me that life moves in seasons—that growth is not hurried, and nothing in creation is rushed or forced. Trees do not strain to bear fruit; they remain rooted and trust the timing of their renewal. Flowers do not bloom on command; they unfold quietly when the time is right. In the stillness of the natural world, I began to understand that stillness does not equal absence. Something sacred is always at work, even when it cannot yet be seen.

The quiet unfolding of creation helped restore my own sense of rhythm and rest. It softened the pressure to "fix" myself and invited me instead to simply be present—to breathe, to notice, to trust. Discernment often came not through striving, but through subtle observation: how a tree endured the wind without losing its ground, how birds launched into the sky without needing to see where they'd land. Their quiet trust mirrored the trust I was learning to cultivate—one rooted not in control, but in surrender.

And then there was connection—simple, trusted presence with those who didn't need me to be fixed or figured out. These weren't people who had answers. They simply listened without judgment, sat with me in silence, and made room for my becoming. Their groundedness helped me find my own.

Over time, I began to realize that this quiet gravitation toward what nourished me—and away from what depleted me—was not just preference. It was spiritual discernment. It was how God began to guide me again—not with loud direction, but through the slow return of sensitivity to what was true, good, and sustaining.

Discernment in the darkness often looks like this: asking small questions and being willing to wait. Taking one step, then listening again. Trusting that God doesn't require certainty—only openness. And believing that He is still leading, even when the path winds slowly.

Hope and discernment didn't just lighten the heaviness. They sharpened my ability to hear and to see. I began to notice the difference between God's voice and the voices of fear, shame, and accusation. I began to make choices not out of panic, but from a place of increasing peace. It wasn't always clear. But I didn't need full clarity. I just needed enough light for the next step. As hope and discernment took root in me, my senses awakened. Not just emotionally, but spiritually. I was no longer just surviving—I was beginning to listen. And God, who had never left me, was gently guiding me all along.

### *Awakening to something new begins with surrender.*

There came a point in my journey when I stopped trying to force my way out of depression. I had prayed, cried, read Scripture, reached for encouragement, and yet the weight lingered. I had done what I knew to do. And still, I felt tired. So I did something unexpected. I stopped striving. I stopped trying to will myself into wholeness. And instead, I surrendered. Not in defeat—but in quiet trust.

I had to let go of my need to understand everything. I released the pressure to get it "right." I laid down the illusion that healing was something I had to achieve. And it was in that space of surrender, empty-handed and uncertain, that I began to awaken. It wasn't dramatic. It was subtle. A flicker of desire to live more fully. A softening of my thoughts. A new way of seeing myself, not through shame, but through God's gentleness. The awakening came as a whisper: *You don't have to fix this. Just be with Me.*

Surrender created room for grace. It opened space for God to move, both around me and within me. And it allowed a different kind of healing to begin, one that wasn't about going back to who I had been, but about becoming someone new.

This awakening wasn't the end of my depression, but it was the beginning of transformation. It was the moment my soul stopped holding its breath. The moment I said, *"Even here, I will trust You."* And with that trust came a sense of hope I hadn't felt in a long time—quiet, steady, and real.

## MOMENTS OF REFLECTION

- Can you recall a moment, however small, when you realized the darkness was beginning to lift? What did it look or feel like?

______________________________________________

______________________________________________

______________________________________________

______________________________________________

❖ What has trust looked like in your life when clarity was absent and the path uncertain?

________________________________________

________________________________________

________________________________________

________________________________________

❖ What forms of "discernment in the dark" or spiritual awakening are you beginning to notice in your own life?

________________________________________

________________________________________

________________________________________

________________________________________

❖ Are there places in your life where God may be inviting you to surrender—not as defeat, but as a doorway to something new?

________________________________________

________________________________________

________________________________________

________________________________________

## CLOSING PRAYER

Dear God of quiet awakenings,
Thank You for the gentle light that grows even in the shadows.
Thank You for finding me in places I thought were forgotten.
When my prayers are silent sighs, You still listen.
When my strength is gone, You still hold me.
When I stop striving, You begin to move—deeply, gently, and faithfully.
Help me recognize Your presence even when it whispers.
Teach me to trust even when the way forward is dim.
Let surrender be the soil where grace takes root.
And when I cannot bloom in the sunlight,
remind me that You have created beauty that grows in the dark, too.
I do not walk this path alone.
And even here, I am becoming.
In Jesus' name I pray. Amen.

### AFFIRMATION

*Even in the shadows, I am not forgotten. I am learning to trust, to surrender, and to awaken. Hope is returning, and discernment is taking place—quietly, steadily, faithfully. The light is in me because God is with me. And even now, something beautiful is beginning to bloom.*

# CHAPTER 6

# Discovery and Insight: The Mind-Body-Spirit Connection

As my healing journey continued, I increasingly understood that recovery from depression is rarely about one thing. There isn't a single cause, nor a single cure. The more I reflected, the more I realized: true healing happens when we tend to the *whole person*—body, mind, and spirit. Healing is facilitated by a series of insights—some quiet, some profound, all meant to change the way we see ourselves. One of the most significant discoveries I made was that, by its very nature, depression tends to weave itself through the entire self—body, mind, and spirit.

We often want a single explanation, a single solution. But healing comes when we begin to see ourselves as whole and beautifully complex. Each part of us carries a piece of our story. Each part of us longs to be heard, understood, and restored.

This chapter explores the integrated nature of healing. It's not about choosing between faith and science, prayer and therapy, or surrender and action. It's about weaving them together, allowing each part of us to be seen, nurtured, and restored.

### *Depression engages a symphony of systems.*

As we've seen in earlier chapters, depression is not confined to emotion—it orchestrates its effects across every part of who we are. It influences the body—disrupting sleep, draining energy, shifting appetite, and even weakening the immune system. It touches the mind—altering how we interpret experiences, how we think about ourselves, and how we imagine the future. And it deeply affects the spirit—dulling our sense of hope, our connection to God and others, and our belief that life still holds purpose.

We are not simple beings. We are intricate, interconnected, *"wonderfully complex"* and *"marvelous"* (Psalm 139:14). God designed us with breathtaking complexity. When one system struggles, others respond. And when one part begins to heal, the others can follow.

In the same way that depression moves through every layer of our being, healing must be layered too. I didn't discover this all at once. It came gradually—through spiritual practices that renewed my hope, therapeutic tools that untangled my thinking, and lifestyle shifts that helped my body rest and recover. Each approach offered something essential. And together, they formed a foundation for deep, lasting healing.

When I began to honor how beautifully I was made—body, mind, and spirit—I also began to care for myself differently. Not out of fear or frustration, but out of reverence. God formed every part of me with intention. And every part of me is worthy of restoration.

### *Therapy complements spiritual insight.*

When I eventually became a therapist myself, I began to understand depression not only from the inside—but also through the lens of those I was called to walk alongside. I came to see how spiritual truths and therapeutic tools are not in competition with one another. They are companions in the journey toward wholeness.

**Cognitive Behavioral Therapy (CBT),** for example, is one of the most researched and effective therapeutic approaches for treating depression. At its core, CBT helps us uncover the patterns of distorted thinking that so often shape our internal world. These aren't just passing thoughts—they're deep-seated beliefs that quietly influence how we view ourselves, others, and even God. Thoughts like *"I'm not enough," "I'll always be this way,"* or *"Nothing will ever change"* may sound familiar. Over time, they become the lens through which we interpret our experiences—reinforcing shame, hopelessness, and despair.

CBT gently invites us to bring these thoughts into the light. It helps us slow down and examine them, to ask: *Is this true? Is this helpful? Is there another way to see this?* It teaches us to challenge false narratives with truth, to reframe our inner dialogue in ways that reflect grace, reality, and hope. Rather than pretending everything is fine or forcing positive thinking, CBT walks us through a process of discovering thoughts that bring life instead of despair. In doing so, it echoes spiritual renewal—what the Apostle Paul called the *"renewing of the mind"* in Romans 12. Through this lens, CBT becomes not just a tool of psychology, but a companion to faith—a way of participating in the sacred work of transformation.

**Mindfulness-based therapy** offers another powerful pathway, especially when our minds feel cluttered or overwhelmed. Where CBT helps us restructure what we think, mindfulness teaches us how to relate to our thoughts differently. It trains us to observe them without judgment, to notice the waves of emotion without getting pulled under by them. In moments of distress, mindfulness invites us to pause instead of react—to breathe, to name what we're feeling, and to stay present to the moment rather than spiral into fear or shame.

This practice may sound modern, but its roots are ancient. Mindfulness shares deep resonance with the contemplative stillness found in prayer, silence, and meditation. When we practice mindfulness, we are not escaping reality—we are entering it more fully, with compassion and awareness. We learn to create space between the stimulus and our response, space where God can meet us, calm us, and remind us of who we are. In this way, mindfulness becomes a spiritual practice—a gentle way of grounding ourselves in the presence of God and the truth that we are not our thoughts. We are beloved, held, and being renewed.

These methods do not replace faith. But they strengthen our ability to live it. Therapy gave language to what I had experienced spiritually: the truth that I am not my thoughts, and I am not alone. I began to see that *renewing the mind* is not only a biblical invitation, but also a lived and layered process that invites us to ". . . *let God transform you into a new person by changing the way that you think" (Romans 12:2).* That transformation isn't always sudden. Sometimes, it comes through the slow work of becoming aware, of releasing old beliefs, and of learning to see ourselves through God's eyes.

Self-awareness and surrender can walk hand in hand. Compassion toward ourselves is not weakness. It's an act of alignment with the heart of God, who sees us clearly and loves us still. Therapy helped me live that truth more fully, one renewed thought at a time.

***Faith opened my spirit to healing—Therapy helped me understand how to live that healing out.***

Together, they became a powerful alliance—one that continues to shape how I offer care, receive grace, and live as someone being restored from the inside out.

***Wholeness is found in the way we live.***

During my healing journey, I began to notice something subtle, yet profound: the way I lived—how I cared for my body, how I structured my days, how I connected with others—was deeply shaping the way I felt. These weren't dramatic changes. They were small shifts. But they mattered.

A quiet walk outside, even for just ten minutes, lifted something heavy inside me. A nourishing meal, made with intention, grounded me more than I expected. A full night of sleep brought clarity that I hadn't felt in weeks. And a single, meaningful conversation reminded me I wasn't alone.

These weren't quick fixes. They didn't erase my depression. But over time, they became steady supports—pillars that helped hold me up as healing took root.

Movement, proper nutrition, rest, and connection are not just physical habits—they are spiritual practices, too. They reflect the kind of gentle stewardship God calls us to as whole beings. We were never meant to compartmentalize our wellness into "spiritual" and "everything else." God created us body, mind, and spirit—and He meets us through every part.

I began to see my body not as a burden or a barrier, but as a companion in healing. When I nourished it, I was honoring the life God had given me. When I rested it, I was trusting Him enough to let go. When I moved it, I was participating in the flow of His sustaining grace.

Wholeness, I learned, doesn't arrive all at once. It is cultivated—in choices, in rhythms, in the way we live our everyday lives. The way we rise, the way we eat, the way we reach out or even slow down—these are not just background details. They are holy invitations.

I discovered three components in my healing and wholeness: prayer and meditation that spoke to my spirit, insight and applicable tools gleaned from therapy, and embracing a gentle way of living with rhythm and reverence for the beautiful, sometimes delicate, and resilient life we've been given.

### *A spiritual foundation of faith informed my approach to body and mind.*

Through every stage of my healing, faith remained the foundation. It wasn't something I turned to only in crisis, nor was it limited to Sunday mornings or morning devotions. It was the rock beneath every other step I took. Prayer, Scripture, silence, worship—these were not just spiritual disciplines; they were lifelines. They reminded me who I was, *whose* I was, and that I was never walking this journey alone.

As I began to integrate physical and emotional healing—through therapy, better nutrition, movement, rest, and self-awareness—my faith didn't diminish. It deepened. It informed everything. It gave context to the choices I was making to care for my whole self.

Jesus spoke of this kind of foundation in Matthew 7:24–25 when He said:

> *"Anyone who listens to my teaching and follows it is wise, like a person who builds a house on solid rock. Though the rain comes in torrents and the floodwaters rise and the winds beat against that house, it won't collapse because it is built on bedrock."*

That passage has taken on new meaning for me. Healing didn't mean the storms stopped. The rain still came—the fatigue, the anxious thoughts, the low days. But I wasn't building my recovery on shifting sand. I was standing on the rock of God's Word, God's presence, and His unchanging love.

Still, even with faith as my foundation, I came to understand that spiritual healing is most effective when it honors the body and mind as well. We are not disjointed beings. God made us integrated—fearfully and wonderfully woven together. Ignoring one part of ourselves, even with good intentions, limits the fullness of the healing God wants to bring.

I began to see that when I ate well, moved my body, rested, or challenged a harmful belief, I wasn't stepping away from my faith—I was living it. Each act of care became an expression of trust. Each rhythm of rest became an act of worship.

Faith taught me that healing is sacred. But it also showed me that healing is holistic. And building that healing on the rock of Christ meant I could withstand more than I imagined—not because I was strong, but because He is.

***Wholeness was never meant to be one-dimensional.***

I didn't find healing from just one source. It came from many directions, converging in ways I couldn't have planned, predicted, or even imagined. It came through prayer whispered in exhaustion. Through journal pages soaked with tears. Through Scripture that found me in silence. Through therapy sessions filled with honesty. Through laughter on days I didn't think I could smile. Through warm meals, deep rest, and unexpected moments of grace. This was not fragmented healing. It was integrated. And in that integration, something deeper began to unfold.

For a long time, I thought healing had to look a certain way—clean, linear, and clearly spiritual. But wholeness doesn't fit into neat categories. It moves through the physical, the emotional, the relational, the intellectual, and the spiritual—all at once, and not always in equal measure. Sometimes it arrives through stillness. Sometimes through movement. Sometimes through Scripture. Sometimes through science.

And I began to see this not as a dilution of my faith, but as a deepening of it.

God was not limited to one method. He was present in *all* of them. I began to recognize Him not only in worship but in the wisdom of a counselor. Not only in quiet time but in the strength gained through proper sleep and nourishment. I felt His grace in moments of stillness, and His compassion through the embrace of community. I even came to see how medication, when needed, could be a vessel of mercy, a way God meets us in our biology as well as our prayers. This realization changed everything. I stopped compartmentalizing my healing and started receiving it.

God is the Author of all truth. The Healer of both body and soul. The Giver of good gifts that come in many forms. And when we allow ourselves to embrace that truth, we stop waiting for one perfect solution and begin welcoming healing wherever it begins to bloom.

Wholeness was never meant to be one-dimensional—because we are not one-dimensional beings. We are layered, beloved, and designed to heal through the wide-open generosity of God.

## MOMENTS OF REFLECTION

❖ In what ways have you seen healing come from more than one source in your life?

❖ Are there areas of your body, mind, or spirit you've unintentionally overlooked in your healing journey?

❖ How has your understanding of faith expanded as you've explored emotional, physical, and relational healing?

❖ What would it look like to embrace healing as a layered, sacred process—one that welcomes God's presence in both prayer and practice?

______________________________

______________________________

______________________________

______________________________

## CLOSING PRAYER

Dear God of wholeness and wonder,
Thank You for designing me with depth and beauty—body, mind, and spirit.
Thank You for being present in the silence,
and in the voices of wise counselors, caring friends,
nourishing meals, quiet walks, and Your sacred Word.
Teach me not to separate the sacred from the practical,
but to see Your fingerprints in them all.
Help me embrace the many ways You bring healing.
You are working in every layer of who I am.
And when I grow weary, remind me again that I do not walk alone.
You are with me, weaving wholeness from all things.
In Jesus' name I pray. Amen.

## AFFIRMATION

*I am healing layer by layer. God meets me in prayer, in practice, and in the daily rhythms of life. Wholeness is unfolding in every part of me.*

# CHAPTER 7

# The Gift of Process: Healing in the Midst of the Unseen

In the chapters leading up to this point, we've explored depression from many angles—its causes, its impact on the whole person, and the spiritual dimension that undergirds our suffering and healing. We've looked at therapies, lifestyle shifts, and spiritual practices that support recovery. But before we move on to practical steps for healing, I want to pause and say this:

***Healing doesn't always come in a straight line.***

Sometimes it unfolds so slowly that we question whether it's happening at all. There may be seasons where the fog doesn't seem to lift, where progress feels painfully imperceptible. We may find ourselves circling back to old patterns, re-encountering familiar sorrows, and wondering, *Am I going backward? Am I failing?*

But here's the truth: *you are not failing—you are forming*. Healing often begins in hidden places, beneath the surface of what others can see and even beneath what we can see ourselves. The process of healing isn't only about feeling better—it's about becoming more whole. And often, that becoming begins where no one is watching.

There is a hidden grace in the process itself, a quiet, steady work of God taking place in the unseen spaces of the soul. It happens in the small choices you make to keep going, to return to prayer, to breathe through the ache, to choose rest when your mind tries to demand productivity. It shows up in the deeper awareness you gain when you pause long enough to listen to your thoughts. It grows in the trust you begin to build, not in outcomes, but in God's presence within the process.

Sometimes healing looks like a breakthrough. But more often, it looks like resilience. It looks like continuing the journey even without visible signs. It looks like faith being formed in silence, like roots growing deep before anything breaks the surface. That is the hidden grace: transformation taking place in the soil of your surrender, watered by your tears, nourished by your persistence, and held by God's unfailing hands. So if you feel stuck, take heart. Beneath the surface, something sacred is unfolding.

***It begins with letting go of the destination.***

When I was in the grip of depression, I clung tightly to the hope of a full and immediate recovery. I longed to "feel like myself" again—to return to some imagined version of wholeness where the heaviness would vanish and clarity would reign. For a while, that longing consumed me. It was the only vision I had for what healing could look like. I imagined that if I could just reach a certain point of healing, even if I didn't know exactly what it was, I would finally feel like myself again.

But over time, something subtle began to shift. I didn't have a sudden revelation, and there was no defining moment. But gradually, my gaze moved from the horizon to the path beneath my feet. I started to notice that I was being shaped, not just in the outcome I was chasing, but in the very act of walking through the valley. Every whispered prayer, every sigh of surrender, every small act of courage to get out of bed or prepare a meal—all of it was forming something deeper in me.

I was no longer waiting for the finish line to define my healing. I began to understand that healing wasn't just what happened when the pain stopped. Rather, it was what happened in the middle of the ache. The sacred work was already underway.

And that shift, from outcome to process, brought with it a new kind of hope. Not the kind tied to future guarantees or emotional milestones, but the kind rooted in God's presence here and now. It was no longer *"I'll be okay when I get through this."* It became *"I am being held even as I walk through this."*

There is beauty in being shaped by the process. When we let go of the need to arrive quickly, we make space for transformation to unfold slowly and more deeply. The process cultivates a kind of wisdom that no quick fix can give. It fosters patience in place of pressure, compassion in place of comparison, trust in place of control. It strips away what is shallow and builds something grounded. In the process, God was forming in me a heart more tender toward others, more present in the moment, and more deeply anchored in truth than I had ever known before.

To be shaped by process is to be shaped from the inside out. And though it often feels slow and unseen, it is never wasted. With every small step, I was being changed, not only in how I felt, but in how I loved, how I listened, and how I lived. And slowly, I discovered a new kind of wholeness, not the kind that erases the past, but the kind that integrates it with grace.

God was not waiting for me at the destination. He was right there walking with me through every step of the journey. And in the very process I once resented, He was already restoring me.

### ***Slow growth is still growth.***

We live in a culture that glorifies speed, quick turnarounds, instant results, measurable milestones. We're conditioned to believe that if we can't see immediate change, then nothing meaningful is happening. But healing doesn't usually work like that. Generally, it rarely makes headlines in our lives. It moves like roots beneath the soil—quiet, hidden, essential.

True healing often begins long before we see evidence of it. Just like a seed planted in the earth, growth starts in the unseen places. Long before the sprout pushes through the surface, roots are forming. Life is stirring in the dark. And the darkness isn't lifeless—it's developmental. What looks like delay is often preparation.

I didn't wake up one day feeling whole or joyful. My healing didn't announce itself with fanfare, clarity, or closure. Instead, it came slowly, in fragments. A single night of deeper sleep. A conversation that didn't drain me. A smile that didn't feel forced. A flicker of energy that reminded me I still had life in me.

At first, I didn't even notice those moments. I was so busy searching for something *bigger*—a sudden breakthrough, a dramatic shift. I initially dismissed the small signs of healing that were already unfolding. But those subtle glimpses were not insignificant. They were the fruit of quiet transformation happening beneath the surface.

Slow growth is still growth. And sometimes, it's the slow kind that takes root the deepest. It teaches us how to be patient with ourselves. It teaches us to trust God, not just for the outcome, but in the becoming.

There's something sacred about this pace. It invites us to stay present. To notice what's already shifting. To release the pressure to "arrive" and instead honor the path we're on. When we accept the slowness of healing, we begin to value things we once overlooked: the courage it takes to rise again, the beauty of resilience in quiet places, and the grace of growing even when no one sees it.

This slower path builds something that quick fixes cannot: Depth. Stability. Wisdom. It makes space for God to do work in us that isn't just about feeling better, but about being transformed.

So if you're still in the dark soil, still wondering when the light will come, take heart. You are not buried. You are being rooted. And even now, new life is reaching toward the surface.

### *There are times when the dark shadows become sacred ground.*

Although I didn't fully realize it at the time, something sacred was taking place, not in spite of the shadows, but within them. I wasn't just waiting to be healed. I was being formed.

Spiritual formation was happening in the unseen, beneath the surface of my suffering. Each quiet surrender, each moment I chose to stay present in my pain instead of running from it, was shaping me. Not instantly. Not obviously. But deeply. It was as if God was rewriting something within me, not loudly, but faithfully.

There's a deep spiritual truth in this: God often does His most transformative work in the shadows. In wilderness places. In seasons of not-knowing, when we cannot trace His hand but still choose to trust His heart. It's in those moments, when clarity is gone and control is out of reach, that trust is forged. Not because we've seen the outcome, but because we've chosen to believe that God is still with us in the mystery.

Psalm 23:4 became a quiet anchor for me: *"Even when I walk through the darkest valley, I will not be afraid, for You are close beside me. Your rod and Your staff protect and comfort me."* This Scripture doesn't promise a path without valleys. It promises that even there, especially there, God is near. Close enough to comfort. Strong enough to protect. Faithful enough to guide.

I began to ask different questions—not *When will I get better?* but *What is God forming in me here?* Not *How can I get through this faster?* but *What is being refined in me through this?* Those questions didn't always yield immediate answers, but they shifted my posture. That curiosity led to insight. The insight led to a strange kind of peace—not because I had resolution, but because I had presence. God's presence.

Over time, that peace made space for healing. Not because the pain vanished, but because it was no longer wasted. It was being held. It was being used. And I was being made new.

I used to think the healing would happen *after* the process—after the tears, the questions, the long nights. But now I see: the process *was* the healing. The very act of showing up each day, of not giving up when it would have been easier to shut down, was holy ground. Every small act of faith was a seed planted in the valley. And God was nurturing something beautiful, something lasting—even there.

### ***The process is the place where faith grows.***

If you find yourself in the in-between—not where you were, but not yet where you long to be—I want to say this gently and clearly: *You are not failing. You are becoming.*

The in-between is sacred space. It may feel uncertain, uncomfortable, or even endless, but it is not empty. It is where trust is formed, where deeper roots take hold, where unseen transformation unfolds. This is the space where faith is not just believed but lived. It's where your soul learns to lean—not on certainty, but on presence. On God's nearness, even when you cannot feel it.

Every breath you take in defiance of despair is holy. Every time you rise when you'd rather stay hidden, every whisper of prayer when words fail, every act of kindness to yourself or others—these are sacred acts. They may seem small, but they are evidence of growth. Evidence that something eternal is being shaped in you.

The process itself is a holy classroom, not a holding cell. You are not being punished—you are being formed. And even if you can't see the fruit yet, the roots are still growing.

Faith doesn't grow because we feel strong. It grows in the quiet, trembling places where we choose to believe—even in our weakness—that God is still at work. That even in the shadows, something good is being formed beneath the surface. We may not feel His hand, but we are not outside His care. The path may feel uncertain, the valley long, but we are not abandoned in it. This is the promise we carry: not that we will always see the way forward, but that we are held and accompanied every step of the way.

So breathe deeply. Be gentle with yourself. Trust the process—even when it looks like nothing is happening. Healing is not only coming; it is already underway.

## MOMENTS OF REFLECTION

❖ Where in your healing journey have you overlooked the growth that was happening beneath the surface?

______________________________________________

______________________________________________

______________________________________________

______________________________________________

❖ What does the "in-between" feel like for you right now? How might it also be sacred space?

______________________________________________

______________________________________________

______________________________________________

______________________________________________

- ❖ How has your faith shifted or deepened, not because you reached a destination, but because you stayed in the process?

________________________________________

________________________________________

________________________________________

________________________________________

- ❖ What small acts of trust are you being invited to take today, even if the outcome is still unseen?

________________________________________

________________________________________

________________________________________

________________________________________

- ❖ How does it comfort you to know that God is close beside you, even in the valley?

________________________________________

________________________________________

________________________________________

________________________________________

## CLOSING PRAYER

Dear God of the in-between,
You are with me in the waiting,
in the not-yet, in the places I don't understand.
Thank You for reminding me that growth is happening even when I can't see it.
Thank You for staying close when I feel far from both You and myself.
Teach me to trust this process—not as punishment,
but as the place where You are forming something deeper in me.
Let every small act of faith become a seed of transformation.
And when I am weary, remind me:
I am not stuck. I am becoming.
In Jesus' name I pray. Amen.

### AFFIRMATION

*I am not failing. I am becoming. Even in the in-between, healing is unfolding within me. God is with me in the process, and my faith is growing—one sacred step at a time.*

# CHAPTER 8

# A Path Less Travelled: Steps Toward Wholeness

I've come to recognize that there is no one-size-fits-all path to healing. No magic formula. No perfectly curated checklist. Healing is not linear, and it rarely follows a script. And yet—there *are* steps we can take. Small, intentional acts of care. Tiny movements toward light. They may not feel like much at first. But taken with faith and honesty, these steps become sacred ground beneath our feet.

For many, the journey out of depression isn't a well-paved highway, clearly marked and easily followed. It's a narrow, winding path, often walked in silence, often hidden from view. It winds through questions we never expected to ask, through nights when hope feels like a flicker, and days when the next step feels impossibly small.

This is what I've come to call *a path less travelled.* Not because few people suffer—but because few people are taught how to heal. And fewer still are encouraged to do so with gentleness, grace, and God.

Choosing to heal, truly heal, is both brave and rare. It takes courage to slow down. It takes resilience to stay present in the ache. It takes trust to keep walking when the way forward is unclear. But every step, however halting or quiet, matters. Healing doesn't usually come all at once. It's made up of moments—moments of honesty, stillness, movement, prayer, and choice.

In this chapter, I don't want to hand you another list of things to "get right." I simply want to offer some gentle guideposts. Consider them companions on the journey—things to hold onto when you forget what healing feels like. You don't have to do them all. You don't have to do them perfectly. But each one may offer a glimmer of light as you take the next step on your path toward wholeness.

### *Step 1: Start Where You Are*

Healing doesn't begin with who you think you *should* be. It begins with who you *are* right now. It begins in the middle of the pain, in the silence, in the quiet stillness, in the uncertainty. It's okay if you feel numb, tired, angry, or stuck. You don't have to pretend to be okay in order to be loved or healed.

I used to think I had to *"feel better"* before I could move forward. I believed that healing required a certain emotional state—one that felt hopeful, strong, or at least a little more put together. But it wasn't until I began naming my actual experience—*I'm sad. I'm scared. I'm exhausted*—that something began to shift. I stopped pretending. I stopped performing. And for the first time, I started receiving.

There is something profoundly healing about naming where we are. Naming is an act of honesty, a way of coming home to ourselves. It doesn't fix everything, but it opens the door to transformation. When we name our pain, we make space for compassion. When we name our fear, we give God something to meet with love. When we name our exhaustion, we give ourselves permission to rest.

The truth is, what remains unnamed often remains unhealed. It lingers in the background, shaping our decisions and depleting our energy. But when we speak it aloud, even in a whisper, we begin to reclaim it. We begin to say: *This is real. This is happening. And I don't have to face it alone.*

Naming your experience doesn't mean you've given up. It means you've chosen to show up—as you truly are, not as you wish to be. It's a significant turning point, a quiet declaration: *I am ready to be honest. I am ready to heal.*

God does not wait for us to be strong before He shows up. He meets us in our weakness, with tenderness and truth. Start where you are. That's where grace will find you.

### *Step 2: Speak Honestly to God*

There is no spiritual script you must follow when you're in pain. You don't need polished prayers, theologically correct language, or perfect words. You only need honesty.

Some of my most sacred prayers during depression were raw and unfiltered. They weren't elegant. They weren't long. Often, they were barely audible. *"Help." "I'm lost." "Don't leave me."* And on some days, even those felt too hard to say. There were only sighs. Tears. Silence.

And still, God was there. Not standing at a distance, waiting for me to say it "right"—but drawing close, listening to the language of my ache. I've come to believe that God listens just as attentively to our groans as to our praise. As Romans 8:26 reminds us, *"But the Holy Spirit prays for us with groanings that cannot be expressed in words."* When you have no words, Heaven still hears.

The Psalms teach us this kind of honesty. They are filled with unfiltered emotion—anguish, longing, rage, despair, doubt, hope. These prayers weren't composed to impress; they were cried out from the depths of human experience. King David didn't shy away from saying, *"How long, O Lord?"* or *"Why have You forsaken me?"* And yet these vulnerable words were preserved as holy.

God's presence is big enough to hold every part of your story—your fears, your confusion, your numbness, your yearning. There is room in His presence for all of it. You don't have to feel close to Him in order to talk to Him. You don't have to understand why you feel the way you do before opening your heart. You don't even have to be sure He'll respond—just speak.

Start from where you are. Not from where you think you "should" be. Your honesty is not a failure of faith. It's the foundation of intimacy. Even if all you can manage is a whisper, that whisper is enough. Even if you can't speak, your tears are enough. Even if you sit in silence, your presence is enough. Remember, God isn't looking for performance. He's looking for presence. He's already near. Speak as you are—and trust that He is already listening.

### *Step 3: Meditate on Life-Giving Scriptures*

Meditation is different from reading for information. It's a way of sitting with truth until it seeps into your bones. During my healing, certain scriptures became lifelines—not because they gave me all the answers, but because they reminded me who God was, even when I couldn't feel Him.

Meditating on Scripture is not about performance. It's about presence. Choose one verse, maybe even a single phrase. Sit with it. Breathe it in. Let it echo. Let it settle over the ache, like balm on a bruise.

A few scriptures became anchors for me. Here are just a few—not as proof texts or quick fixes, but as gentle companions:

- *"The Lord is close to the brokenhearted; He rescues those whose spirits are crushed."* (Psalm 34:18)
- *"Come to me, all of you who are weary and carry heavy burdens, and I will give you rest"* (Matthew 11:28)

- *"Give all your worries and cares to God, for He cares about you."* (I Peter 5:7)

Let one verse be enough. Read it slowly. Whisper it aloud. Write it down and carry it with you. Let the truth work on you—not by your effort, but by grace.

### *Step 4: Shift One Thought*

Our thoughts don't always tell the truth, but they often shape the way we see ourselves, others, and even God. In the fog of depression, thoughts can become loops of fear, shame, or despair. Trying to change every thought can feel impossible. But shifting just *one* can open a door.

Start small. Ask yourself gently: *Is this thought true? Is it kind? Is it from God?* If not, is there another thought—even just slightly more hopeful—you can choose instead?

Our thoughts shape our experience more than we often realize. In the fog of depression, thoughts can become automatic and consuming—deep grooves in the mind that reinforce despair, shame, or hopelessness. Left unchecked, they can steer us away from healing and into deeper darkness. That's why it's so important to not just notice our thoughts, but to challenge them with intention and grace.

This doesn't mean forcing positivity or pretending everything is okay. It means recognizing when a thought is doing harm—and gently redirecting it toward something more constructive. We're not talking about blind optimism.

We're talking about choosing thoughts that lead toward life rather than away from it.

One of my earliest shifts was from *"I'll never get out of this"* to *"Maybe I'm not as stuck as I feel."* It was a small change, but it mattered. That single adjustment didn't make everything better, but it softened despair's grip. It gave me space to breathe. It reminded me that my current feeling wasn't the whole truth, and that even in my lowest place, there was still room for light to break in.

Thoughts can either become prison walls or stepping stones. And we have more power than we realize to shape the narrative we live inside. Constructive thinking doesn't deny pain—it gives it context. It says, *"Yes, I'm hurting—but healing is possible. Yes, I feel stuck—but this moment doesn't define me. Yes, I'm overwhelmed—but I can take one small step."*

Choosing to challenge our thoughts is an act of courage. It's a way of saying, *"I will not let despair speak the final word."* It's a practice of aligning our minds with truth, kindness, and hope—one quiet, redemptive thought at a time.

Philippians 4:8 gives us a sacred framework for how to guide our minds toward healing: "*Fix your thoughts on what is true, and honorable, and right, and pure, and lovely, and admirable. Think about things that are excellent and worthy of praise."* This doesn't mean forcing positivity or denying pain. It means choosing, when we're able, to notice where beauty, truth, and goodness still live—even in the struggle. Even the smallest shift toward light can make space for healing. Every thought we reshape is a quiet act of trust. And every time we choose truth over despair, we step closer to wholeness.

### *Step 5: Listen to Music That Speaks to the Soul*

Music has the ability to reach places in us that words alone cannot. During my depression, there were days when Scripture felt distant and prayer felt hollow—but a song could still move something inside me. It bypassed my defenses. It softened the numbness. It became a kind of prayer when I had no words.

Whether it's worship, instrumental, or a song with lyrics that speak gently of longing and hope, music has a way of creating space for emotion, for presence, for healing. Don't underestimate its power. Let yourself be ministered to by melody. Let lyrics remind you of truth. Let the sound carry what your heart cannot express.

### *Step 6: Do One Small Thing*

When you're in the depths of depression, even the simplest tasks can feel insurmountable. Things that once felt effortless—getting dressed, brushing your teeth, making a meal—suddenly require energy you don't have and motivation you can't muster. It's not laziness. It's the weight of hopelessness pressing down so heavily that the ordinary becomes monumental. That's why small steps matter so much. Doing one small thing in the midst of depression isn't insignificant—it's defiant. It's an act of quiet resistance against despair. It's a way of saying, *I may not feel strong, but I am still here. I am still choosing life, one breath, one movement, one moment at a time.*

Take a shower. Open the blinds and let the light in. Sit by a window with a warm drink and just breathe. Step outside and feel the air on your face. Make a simple, nourishing meal—not because you're hungry, but because your body deserves care. Text a friend, even just to say "thinking of you." Fold the laundry, water the plants, change the sheets. These aren't just tasks on a to-do list. They're declarations: *I'm not giving up. I'm participating in my healing, even if it's one small gesture at a time.*

Every small act becomes a seed of restoration. And God sees every one. Not a single effort is wasted. The Bible reminds us that *"He will not crush the weakest reed or put out a flickering candle."* (Isaiah 42:3). That means even your weakest flame is still light. Even your faintest movement toward life is honored.

In seasons like these, small doesn't mean unimportant. It means sustainable. Gentle. Attuned to your real capacity. And over time, those small steps begin to build something steady—something that tells your body and soul, *You're still alive. You're still becoming. You are worth showing up for.* Start small. Stay gentle. And know that each quiet act of care is holy ground.

### *Step 7: Spend Time in Nature*

Nature became one of my most consistent therapists. There was something deeply healing about being among trees, near water, or simply walking slowly under an open sky. I wasn't trying to accomplish anything. I was just being. And in that being, something in me began to settle.

Spending time in nature—often called *ecotherapy*—has been shown to reduce symptoms of depression and anxiety. But beyond the science, it offers spiritual recalibration. Nature teaches us rhythm. It teaches us surrender. It reminds us that life moves, seasons change, and we are part of something larger.

You don't have to hike a mountain. Just step outside. Breathe in fresh air. Listen to the birds singing. Let sunlight fall on your skin like a benediction. The earth holds a kind of quiet wisdom—if we slow down enough to receive it.

### *Step 8: Let Others In*

Depression has a way of trying to convince us to retreat. It tells us that we're too much, too messy, too broken to be understood. It whispers lies like *"No one wants to hear this"* or *"You'll only be a burden."* But those are the voices of isolation, not truth. And healing was never meant to be walked alone.

From the beginning, we were created for connection—not as an optional comfort, but as an essential part of being human. *"It is not good for man to be alone"* was God's first declaration about human need. And that truth still stands.

Isolation may feel safer in the short term, but it stifles the very light we're trying to find again.

I know how vulnerable it can feel to reach out, especially when you're already fragile. When your energy is low and your confidence is even lower. When shame has set up residence in your soul. But even the smallest step toward connection can begin to break the silence.

Letting someone in doesn't mean you have to explain everything. It doesn't mean you have to be eloquent or put together. It simply means being willing to say, *"I'm struggling."* Or even, *"Can we just sit together today?"*

You don't need someone to fix you. You need someone to *witness* you—to hold space for your pain without judgment, to sit with you in the quiet, to remind you gently that you are not alone.

That someone might be a trusted friend who listens well. It might be a counselor who understands the terrain of emotional struggle. It might be a pastor, mentor, or support group who can walk beside you in faith. Whoever it is, the point is not perfection—it's presence. Even one safe relationship can become a lifeline.

Let someone in—even just a little. It doesn't have to be all at once. It can be a single conversation, a short message, an honest answer to *"How are you?"* That opening may feel small, but in the realm of healing, it's significant.

Connection is one of the places where God loves to dwell. And when we let others into our suffering, we often find, much to our surprise, that grace comes with them.

Sometimes in words, sometimes in silence, but always in love.

Again, let others in; you were never meant to heal alone. Let someone help you remember who you are when you've forgotten. Let someone help to carry part of the weight. Let someone see you—and still stay.

### *Step 9: Rebuild a Sense of Rhythm*

When everything inside feels disoriented—when your thoughts race, your energy dips unpredictably, and your sense of time blurs—rhythm can become one of the most healing gifts you offer yourself. Not a strict schedule or a productivity plan, but a *gentle rhythm*—one that creates a sense of steadiness when everything else feels unsteady.

Rhythms aren't about doing more. They're about coming back to center. They are the quiet structures that whisper to your nervous system: *You are safe. You are anchored. You are not drifting.*

For me, it began with small, deliberate choices. Waking up at the same time each morning—not to seize the day, but to remind myself that I was still part of it. Drinking water with intention. Preparing a simple meal and blessing it with gratitude. Lighting a candle during prayer time, marking that moment as sacred. Sitting outside—even for five or ten minutes—to feel sunlight on my skin or hear the wind move through the trees. These weren't grand acts. They were sacred repetitions. Tiny rituals of presence and peace. And over time, they became anchors that helped stabilize the storm inside.

When we are depressed or anxious, life can feel like it's unraveling, inside and out. Days blur together. Motivation disappears. Energy comes and goes without warning. In those seasons, rhythm becomes a form of care. A way to reintroduce gentleness. A way to build internal and external scaffolding so that healing has space to grow. Even the simplest acts can be powerful:

- Making your bed in the morning.
- Journaling before bed.
- Stretching your body for five minutes.
- Lighting a lamp or candle at dusk to honor the close of the day.
- Reading a Psalm or listening to music that calms your spirit.

These rhythms are not about performance. They are about presence. They give your body and soul a pattern to rest in. A signal that life is still moving forward. That you are participating, even in small ways.

In the midst of healing, rhythm becomes a spiritual practice. A way to slow down and say, *I am still here. I am still worthy of care.* A way to live as if healing is indeed happening—even on the days when you can't yet feel it.

You don't have to do everything at once. Choose one

rhythm that feels accessible. Let it become your grounding place. Then, as strength returns, allow that rhythm to expand. Healing is rarely loud. Often, it begins with these quiet, repeated choices—patterns of care that remind you, again and again, that your life is worth tending to.

### *Step 10: Trust the Slowness*

Of all the steps, this may be the most counterintuitive—and the most courageous: *to trust that healing doesn't have to be fast to be real.* We live in a culture that celebrates urgency. We're taught to chase results, track milestones, and fix what's broken as quickly as possible. But the soul doesn't heal on a schedule. And depression rarely responds to pressure. It asks something different from us—something more tender and brave. It asks us to slow down.

Slowness is not stagnation. It's not failure. It's not a lack of faith. Slowness, in the context of healing, is sacred. It makes space for the unseen. It allows transformation to take root below the surface, where the deepest work often happens.

Healing doesn't always look like progress. Sometimes it looks like rest. Like repetition. Like returning to the same simple practice day after day, even when it feels fruitless. Sometimes it looks like stillness, or tears that return for no clear reason, or a quiet endurance that says, *I'm still here.*

Just like seeds planted in the earth, healing often happens underground first. Invisible to others. Sometimes even invisible to us. But life is stirring. Roots are stretching. Soil is shifting. And in time—when conditions are right—something will break through. Not because we forced it, but because we honored the pace of growth.

I remember days when I felt like nothing was changing. When I questioned whether all the effort, all the prayers, all the quiet acts of hope were making any difference at all. But looking back, I see now: those were the days when something holy was happening. When God was doing the hidden work. When my soul was being prepared to hold more light.

This kind of trust isn't flashy. It's not a dramatic leap. It's a steady return. It's choosing life in small, faithful ways. It's lighting a candle when the room still feels dim. It's whispering a prayer when your heart still feels heavy. It's believing that God is near, even when you feel numb to His presence.

You don't have to feel progress to be in the process of healing. You don't have to see the fruit to know the seed is growing. Trust the slowness. Trust the gentle unfolding. Trust that God is doing something sacred in the soil of your soul—even now. Because in the Kingdom of God, slowness is not wasted. It's where depth is formed. It's where roots are strengthened. And it's where grace meets us—patiently, tenderly, without demand.

Let the fruit come in His time. Your job is not to force the growth. It's to remain open. To stay present. To believe, even in the quiet, that you are still becoming.

### ***Your path forward is not a race, but a gentle unfolding.***

The steps shared in this chapter are not instructions to follow in perfect order, but invitations to explore as you're able. Some days you may take a step forward. Other days you may need to pause and rest. That's okay. This path was never meant to be rushed. It was meant to be lived—with kindness, courage, and the quiet trust that even small movements matter.

You may not feel like you're becoming whole. But wholeness is not a feeling. It is a direction. And every time you choose presence over avoidance, honesty over hiding, grace over shame—you are walking in that direction.

Remember, you are not walking alone. As you continue, hold these gentle truths close:

- You don't have to feel strong to be in the process of healing.
- You don't have to move quickly to be making progress.
- You don't have to have all the answers to be held by God.
- You don't have to be finished to be loved.

Let this be enough for today: that you showed up. That you read these words. That you are still here. You are still becoming. And that is sacred.

## MOMENTS OF REFLECTION

- ❖ Which of the ten steps most speaks to where you are right now? Why?

______________________________________________

______________________________________________

______________________________________________

______________________________________________

- ❖ What is one small, kind thing you can do today to care for yourself?

______________________________________________

______________________________________________

______________________________________________

______________________________________________

- ❖ Are there thoughts or beliefs you've been holding that could be gently challenged with truth?

______________________________________________

______________________________________________

______________________________________________

______________________________________________

- What makes it difficult for you to trust the slowness of your healing process? What might help you release the pressure?

________________________________________

________________________________________

________________________________________

________________________________________

- Who is one safe person you could let in, even just a little? What might that look like?

________________________________________

________________________________________

________________________________________

________________________________________

## CLOSING PRAYER

Dear God of the steady and slow,
Thank You for not rushing me.
Thank You for calling every small step sacred,
and for honoring the quiet ways I choose to keep going.
When I feel like I'm not making progress,
remind me that healing isn't always visible.
When I grow weary of waiting, remind me that You are still working.

When I forget the power of small things—
the shower taken, the window opened, the prayer whispered—
remind me that You see it all.
And that You are proud of me.
Help me to move forward with gentleness,
to think with compassion, to rest without guilt,
and to trust the slow miracle of becoming whole.
I offer You my tiredness and my hope.
Thank You for walking with me, step by step.
In Jesus' name I pray. Amen.

**AFFIRMATION**

*I don't have to do everything at once. Every small step I take is sacred. I am healing—slowly, steadily, and with grace. God is walking with me, and I am still becoming.*

# CHAPTER 9

# Transformation Along the Way: From Pain to Purpose

I didn't begin this journey looking for transformation. I wasn't searching for meaning. I just wanted to feel better. I wanted the heaviness to lift, the fog to clear, and life to feel livable again. I wanted the ache to ease and the silence to break. I longed for relief—that's it, nothing more, nothing less.

But somewhere along the way, something unexpected began to take shape. I began to notice that my pain wasn't just something to escape—it was also something that was forming me. It opened doors I hadn't known were there. It softened parts of me that had grown guarded, even rigid. It deepened my empathy for others who suffer in silence. It gave me the words to express my pain, helped me see compassion more clearly, and made me more aware of the hidden hurts people carry.

And perhaps most unexpectedly, my pain began to whisper of purpose. Let me be clear: *pain itself is not purpose.* Depression, in its most brutal form, is a kind of suffering that defies tidy meanings and easy takeaways. Pain is pain. It can crush, isolate, and disorient. But when healing begins—when light begins to return—something else can emerge: the unfolding of a divine work.

We begin to see that purpose is not always found in *spite* of the pain, but often through it. Not because the pain was good, but because God is good—and He wastes nothing. He redeems even what we could never have chosen.

What I found was not just recovery—it was transformation. A new way of seeing, feeling, listening, and living. Not because I became someone else, but because I became more fully myself.

### *Depression often works as a refining fire.*

There are certain qualities that suffering seems to cultivate—compassion, humility, empathy, resilience, and spiritual depth. These virtues aren't born in ease. They are formed slowly, painfully, in places we would never choose to go. They're shaped in the fire.

Looking back, I can see how depression became a kind of crucible in my life. It didn't just break me—it refined me. It burned away that false sense of strength I had and forced me to confront the layers I had long avoided. It dismantled the illusion that I was in control, that I could fix everything with effort or faith alone.

In that fire, my old assumptions fell apart. My identity, once rooted in performance or certainty, was stripped to its core. And though the process was excruciating, it made space for something more authentic to emerge—something more grounded, more surrendered, more *alive*.

This didn't happen quickly. And there was no one moment of arrival. The refining was slow, almost imperceptible. But it was real. And it changed me—not just how I felt, but how I lived.

Depression didn't just strip away the excess—it clarified what could truly endure. The false supports I had leaned on—self-reliance, productivity, perfectionism—were gradually dismantled. What remained was raw, honest, and unexpectedly authentic. Depression didn't make me less of who I was; it made room for me to discover who I had been all along beneath the striving. It tested the foundation of my faith, my identity, and my strength—and though I wavered, I found that grace held me when nothing else could.

In the fire of that refining season, I encountered a version of myself I hadn't known before. Not the polished self I tried to present, but the real one—tender, surrendered, and rooted in something deeper than performance. I wasn't being undone—I was being remade. What I thought was the end of my strength was the beginning of a different kind of strength and resilience. One not born of effort, but of rest. Not forged in certainty, but in trust. A strength shaped by surrender.

### ***Something miraculous unfolded when I stopped striving—I became.***

For much of my life, I understood calling as something I had to achieve. It was measured by what I could do, the roles I held, the goals I accomplished, the ways I served. I carried an unspoken belief that value was tied to output—that being useful to God meant being busy for God. But depression interrupted that story. It stripped away my capacity to perform. It silenced the rhythm of doing and left me face-to-face with questions I could no longer avoid: *Who am I when I'm not accomplishing anything? What remains when the titles fall away? What is God doing in me—not just through me?*

For a while, I didn't have answers. But over time, in the quiet aftermath of striving, something miraculous began to unfold: *I started to become.* Not someone new, exactly—but someone more true. Someone shaped not by applause or achievement, but by grace. Someone softened by pain, deepened by silence, and awakened to a calling that was no longer performance-driven, but presence-rooted.

I began to see that my experience of depression was not a detour—it was formation. It wasn't a pause in my purpose; it was a part of it. Through suffering, I was being refined—not disqualified, but repurposed.

I discovered that purpose isn't always about platform or

position. Sometimes, it's simply about presence. Showing up. Offering compassion forged in fire. Listening with tenderness born from personal ache. Letting others know they're not alone.

In the stillness where I thought everything had ended, God was quietly rewriting my understanding of calling. He was teaching me that becoming is holy work. And that in Him, I didn't have to strive—I only had to be.

### *Your pain holds power and purpose.*

If you're still in the middle of your pain, the idea of purpose may feel distant—or even offensive. I understand. You may not be ready to talk about meaning. And that's okay. Healing does not require us to make sense of our suffering before we're ready. There is no need to rush toward answers.

But even if you can't see it now, hold this quietly in your heart: *your pain holds power.* Not because pain is good, but because God is good—and He does not waste a single tear. He doesn't dismiss your doubts, your silence, or your aching questions. He gathers it all. And in time, He redeems it.

You may not see it yet, but there may come a day when your story becomes someone else's lifeline. When the empathy you gained through suffering becomes the exact balm someone else needs. When the insight born in your valley becomes light for someone else's path.

You don't have to have it all figured out. You don't need to be "on the other side." What you're living—even now—is part of a divine unfolding. The truth is, your pain has not disqualified you—it has *deepened* you. It has given you wisdom that cannot be taught in a classroom. It has rooted your compassion in real soil. It has formed a kind of strength that doesn't shout but quietly stands with those who suffer.

This is not the power the world celebrates. It's the power of Christ at work in the hidden places, the kind that heals from the inside out and brings beauty from ashes. You are being shaped for something more enduring, more compassionate, and more alive than you ever imagined.

### *Depression brings with it a cloud of witnesses.*

The journey through depression can feel isolating, but you are not alone. Across time, cultures, and contexts, others have walked through the valley of despair and emerged—slowly, painfully, and courageously into lives of deeper meaning and compassion. They are part of what Scripture calls a *cloud of witnesses* (Hebrews 12:1)—those who have gone before us, bearing the weight of sorrow and now bearing witness to healing.

Their stories don't erase the pain. They don't tie it up with a bow. But they remind us that transformation is possible. That beauty can rise from ashes. That purpose can be born, not in spite of suffering, but often through it. Consider the following Biblical, historical, and contemporary examples.

**Elijah: A Prophet Who Sat Under a Tree**

In 1 Kings 19, we meet the prophet Elijah not in triumph, but in collapse. After standing boldly for truth, he flees into the wilderness, exhausted and afraid. Under a broom tree, he prays not for strength—but for death. *"I have had enough, Lord,"* he says. *"Take my life."*

And yet, God does not chastise him. He feeds him. He lets him rest. He draws near in a whisper. And He sends him back—not in shame, but in renewed calling. Elijah's pain was not the end of his story. It was the place where God met him in tenderness and prepared him for what was next.

**Paul: A Disciple Who Despaired of Life Itself**

In 2 Corinthians 1:8, the Apostle Paul speaks openly of a time when he and his companions were *"crushed and overwhelmed beyond our ability to endure, and we thought we would never live through it."* These are not words of spiritual weakness—they are words of human honesty.

Throughout his letters, Paul describes personal anguish, conflict, persecution, and what he called *"a thorn in my flesh."* (2 Corinthians 12:7). While we don't know exactly what this thorn was, it impacted him deeply—and he pleaded for its removal. But God's response was not healing in the way Paul expected. It was a deeper promise: *"My grace is all you need. My power works best in weakness."* (2 Corinthians 12:9). His story reminds us that despair is not incompatible with faith. In fact, his most transformative theology came not from certainty, but from surrender. His pain shaped his message—and his message became a lifeline for the suffering.

**Abraham Lincoln: A Leader Formed by Sorrow**

Before he became one of history's most revered presidents, Abraham Lincoln endured a lifetime of profound sadness. Historians widely agree that he struggled with what we would now call clinical depression. Friends often worried for his well-being during his darkest seasons. He once wrote, *"I am now the most miserable man living."* And yet, it was precisely this depth of feeling that made him a president capable of moral clarity and empathy. He led a fractured nation through civil war and slavery, not from a place of invincibility, but from a well of hard-won humility.

Lincoln's sorrow became soil for his wisdom. His depression didn't disqualify him—it refined his leadership. He reminds us that even those who lead nations can carry great pain—and still carry great purpose.

**Allie Brosh: Drawing Light in the Dark**

Allie Brosh, creator of *Hyperbole and a Half*, opened a window into the interior world of depression through her simple yet profound illustrated stories. With raw honesty and quiet humor, she described what it feels like to lose interest in everything and still hope for something better.

Her work became a mirror for millions who saw

themselves in her words. What began as a personal struggle became a collective voice. By drawing the darkness as it truly was, Allie helped others name their own—and in doing so, offered light.

### Elizabeth Wurtzel: Writing Truth into the Silence

With *Prozac Nation*, Elizabeth Wurtzel became one of the first authors to speak openly and unapologetically about living with clinical depression. Her writing was bold, messy, and deeply human. She didn't claim to have overcome everything—she simply told the truth.

In doing so, she helped tear down the walls of stigma. Her voice gave others the courage to speak, to seek help, and to believe that their pain didn't make them unlovable. Her legacy isn't perfection—it's presence. Her honesty became a healing invitation.

### Anna Akana: Creating from Grief

After her sister's suicide, Anna Akana was lost in grief and depression. She didn't find healing overnight—but she found a spark in unexpected places. Comedy. Storytelling. Creative expression. Over time, Anna built a platform through YouTube and performance where she could process her pain and connect with others.

She turned tragedy into testimony—not by denying the pain, but by honoring it. Her art became a place where others could laugh, cry, and feel seen. And through it, she became a voice for mental health awareness and hope.

**Meri Nana-Ama Danquah: Illuminating the Shadows**

Meri Nana-Ama Danquah, a Ghanaian-American writer, offered one of the pioneering voices on depression within the African American community through her memoir, *Willow Weep for Me: A Black Woman's Journey Through Depression.* In this groundbreaking work, Danquah candidly shares her personal battle with clinical depression, a condition often stigmatized and misunderstood, particularly in Black communities.

By articulating her struggles, she not only confronted her own pain but also challenged the pervasive silence surrounding mental health in African American culture. Her courage to speak out has paved the way for others to seek help and has fostered a broader dialogue on the intersection of race, gender, and mental health.

Each story and testimony above, whether biblical, historical, or contemporary, serves as a beacon, illuminating the possibility of transformation through the crucible of depression. Each of these lives adds to the witness—proof that depression, though devastating, does not get the final word. Healing, though slow, is possible. That God is not done writing ***your*** story.

Though the contemporary individuals named above may not all speak from a Christian perspective, there's no denying that their honesty shines light into dark places. Their courage to speak openly reminds us that healing often begins when silence ends. As believers, we hold to a deeper hope: "The light shines in the darkness, and the darkness can never extinguish it" (John 1:5). These stories, though varied in voice, reflect glimpses of that same light.

You may not feel like a witness yet. You may still be walking through your own valley. But you are not alone. Others have been here. Others have become. And you are becoming, too.

## MOMENTS OF REFLECTION

❖ Where have you begun to notice transformation in your own life, even if it's small or slow?

________________________________________

________________________________________

________________________________________

________________________________________

❖ How has your pain shaped your empathy, your voice, or your view of others who suffer?

________________________________________

________________________________________

________________________________________

________________________________________

❖ What would it mean to release the idea of performance and embrace becoming?

______________________________________________

______________________________________________

______________________________________________

______________________________________________

❖ Are there parts of your story that you once felt ashamed of, but now see as meaningful?

______________________________________________

______________________________________________

______________________________________________

______________________________________________

❖ Which witness in this chapter speaks to something in your own journey?

______________________________________________

______________________________________________

______________________________________________

______________________________________________

## CLOSING PRAYER

Dear God of becoming,
Thank you for not wasting my pain.
You meet me in the shadows,
and You call me by name gently toward the light.
When I wanted relief, You offered transformation.
When I thought my story was over,
You whispered that it was only just unfolding.
Thank You for the cloud of witnesses who have gone before me—
those who sat in silence, even wept in valleys,
and yet found You to be faithful.
Continue to shape me through my struggles,
not into someone else, but into who You created me to be.
Let my scars speak of Your healing,
and my voice become a sound of comfort to others.
And when I forget the purpose hidden in the process,
please remind me that I am still becoming.
In Jesus' name I pray. Amen.

### AFFIRMATION

*My pain is not wasted. My story is not over. I am still becoming. I am shaped by grace, rooted in truth, and held in the hands of a faithful God.*

# CHAPTER 10

# The Path of No Return: Sustaining the Light

There comes a point in the healing journey when something shifts—not all at once, but undeniably. The heaviness begins to lift. You find yourself breathing more deeply. A laugh escapes your lips when you least expect it. You catch yourself noticing beauty again—sunlight filtering through the trees, the rhythm of a song, the comfort of a loved one's voice.

You realize you're no longer just surviving—you're beginning to live again. It's a sacred and tender moment. One that brings relief, and also a new kind of vulnerability: *How do I stay here? How do I protect what's been restored?*

This chapter isn't about creating pressure to "stay healed" or to never struggle again. It's about learning to **sustain the light** that has returned—through rhythms of care, sacred disciplines, and intentional presence. It's about building a life that honors your wholeness and holds space for your humanity. One where you don't strive for perfection but cultivate resilience. One where you know how to return to the light, even if the shadows pass by again.

The truth is this: There may still be hard days. There may still be moments when the old ache whispers or when fatigue settles in. But something has changed: *you have changed.*

You've walked through the darkness. You've encountered grace in the silence. You've tasted freedom. And now, you are walking a path of no return—not because you'll never struggle again, but because you are no longer the same person who entered the valley empty-handed.

You are no longer empty-handed. You carry light now. You carry wisdom. You carry the memory of every moment God sustained you when you didn't think you could go on. You carry His faithfulness in your bones. And with it, you carry something else—*resilience.* Not the kind shaped by self-sufficiency or forced strength, but the kind forged in the fire of surrender. The kind built one gentle step at a time, through tears, through silence, through trust.

This is the journey of sustaining—not arriving but abiding. Not striving but remaining grounded. Resilience now walks beside you, not as a goal to reach, but as a grace that allows you to live from healing to healing, not merely chase after it.

***Resilience is rooted in rhythm.***

Resilience isn't built in moments of urgency—it's cultivated over time, through steady rhythms of care. We often think of resilience as something we either have or don't, something summoned in a crisis. But the truth is, it's formed in the quiet routines, the repeated returns to what restores us. It's not about being strong all the time. It's about returning—again and again—to what brings you back to center.

These rhythms don't need to be grand or complicated. They just need to be life-giving. Think of them as your anchors—daily patterns that gently root your body, mind, and spirit in stability and grace. Here are a few examples of these quiet anchors:

- **A moment of prayer, meditation, or reflection each morning**, to invite God into your day before the world demands your attention
- **Nourishing meals**, not just for fuel but as acts of care and presence
- **Movement**, whether through walking, stretching, dancing, or simply breathing deeply with intention
- **Time in nature**, letting creation speak calm and beauty into your spirit
- **Consistent, restful sleep**, as a foundational act of trust and renewal
- **Meaningful connection**, even brief, with people who remind you that you matter
- **Journaling or stillness**, creating space to process, notice, and breathe

These are not obligations. They are invitations—ways of telling your nervous system, your spirit, and your soul: *You are safe. You are valued. You are supported.*

In the same way that trauma can dysregulate and fragment, rhythm helps restore and reconnect. It creates internal safety. It says to your body and soul: *We're not in survival mode anymore. We are healing now.*

These daily acts, however small, are the foundation of sustained wellness. They remind you of what's true when emotions shift or life gets loud. And over time, they become habits of hope.

Resilience doesn't mean you'll never feel low again. It means you've built a structure that holds you when you do. And that structure is shaped one sacred rhythm at a time.

### *Staying Spiritually Grounded Sustains Us on All Levels.*

As healing deepens, it becomes clear that true wellness is not just emotional or physical—it's also spiritual. When we stay spiritually grounded, we create a foundation that supports every other part of us. Our minds find clarity. Our emotions gain perspective. Our bodies respond to the steadiness of peace. We are sustained from the inside out.

In my own life, spiritual practices have become more than rituals to check off or disciplines to master. They have become lifelines—consecrated spaces of return where I reconnect with myself and re-enter the presence of God.

These practices are not about performance; they are about presence. They are the quiet roots that keep me anchored when the winds rise, the steady rhythm beneath the noise of daily life. I do not engage them perfectly—far from it. But what matters most is not perfection. It's consistency. It's the willingness to return.

When my thoughts spiral or when old shadows knock at the door, it's these rhythms that help me come back to center. A whispered prayer. A promise of Scripture spoken aloud. A few moments of stillness with my hand on my heart. Lighting a candle before journaling. These small acts draw me back to God—not because they guarantee peace, but because they create space for it. And often, it's in that space—simple, quiet, undramatic—that I remember who I am and whose I am.

These practices do not remove all struggle, but they change the posture of my soul. They re-orient me toward truth. They remind me that I don't have to carry everything alone. That I am held. That God is near. Over time, I've come to see these moments not as interruptions to real life, but as the very ground that sustains it.

Prayer is no longer just a plea for help—it has become a steady rhythm, a continual conversation with the One who knows me fully and loves me anyway. Scripture speaks to me differently now. It's not just instruction; it's nourishment for my soul. It reminds me of what is true when my thoughts are scattered. Worship is a way I realign with God's presence, and gratitude softens my heart when anxiety tries to harden it.

These spiritual rhythms are not meant to be burdens. They are meaningful lifelines. Invitations, not obligations. They whisper, *"Come back. Sit down. Be still. Remember that you are not alone."*

Because we are whole beings—body, mind, and spirit—what we practice in our spiritual lives ripples into every other part of us. These sacred rhythms are not only acts of worship; they are acts of restoration. Time with God calms our nervous systems, offering a safe place for our bodies to exhale the tension they so often carry. Stillness settles our racing thoughts, gently reminding our minds that they don't have to have all the answers. Truth shines light into the dark corners of distortion, calling out the lies we've believed and replacing them with the steady voice of grace. And grace—always grace—interrupts the shame that tries to cling to us, speaking a deeper word: You are loved. You are seen. You are still becoming.

These are not empty practices or mere traditions. They are lifelines, woven into the fabric of our healing. They don't just make us feel more spiritual—they make us more human. More rooted. More alive. They awaken us to God's presence not just in moments of devotion, but in every ordinary space of our lives. Over time, they help us live less from reaction and more from remembrance—remembrance that we are held, that we are whole, and that the sacred and the everyday are not so far apart.

It's here, in these small faithful returns, that we begin to live into the reality Paul spoke of: "For in Him we live and move and exist" (Acts 17:28). Our very existence—our breath, our steps, our becoming—is rooted in Him. Healing, like faith, is not a destination but a way of living in deeper awareness of the One who holds us.

When we nurture these habits, we are not just "doing spiritual things"—we are becoming more present to the life God has given us, more attuned to His voice, and more anchored in the truth that healing, like faith, is lived out one small, blessed moment at a time. And as we return again and again to these rhythms of grace, we find ourselves not striving, but abiding—in Him, and in the healing He so faithfully unfolds.

Sustaining the light means making space for God daily—not just in crisis, but in the ordinary. It means staying rooted even when the winds are calm so that when storms come, your anchor already holds. When you stay spiritually grounded, you carry peace into every room you enter—even the dark ones. You are less easily shaken. And even when you are, you know how to return. Not by striving, but by abiding.

### *Healing deepens in the presence of safe connection.*

Depression often isolates us. It wraps us in invisible walls, convincing us that we are too much, too broken, or too burdensome to be loved or understood. It feeds the lie that no one could truly meet us in our weakness, so we learn to retreat—to hide the tender places of our hearts even from ourselves.

But healing calls us differently. It does not shout or demand; it gently coaxes us out of the places where fear has kept us bound. Healing doesn't come with pressure—it comes with a whisper, soft and persistent, inviting us into connection again. It speaks to the deepest longing within us: *You don't have to do this by yourself.*

True healing reminds us that isolation is not our destiny. It reminds us that being seen, known, and loved is part of how God designed us to heal. It assures us that we are not burdens to be tolerated, but lives to be cherished. It is in safe connection—whether with a friend, a counselor, a faith community, a support group, or God Himself—that the walls around our hearts begin to loosen. And as we step, even timidly, toward others, we discover a profound truth: *healing was always meant to be a shared journey, not a solitary path.*

We were created for connection. From the very beginning, humanity was designed to live in relationship—with Him and with each other. And when we walk through pain, those relationships become lifelines. Not because others can fix us, but because they can remind us that we still matter. Healing is holy—and so is companionship. We need people who can hold space for our process. People who will sit with us in silence, speak truth when we forget it, and celebrate even our smallest steps forward.

Jesus said, *"For where two or three gather together as my followers, I am there among them."* (Matthew 18:20). That promise isn't just for church services—it's for every living room, hospital room, and coffee shop where someone shares their truth and is met with grace. When we gather—even with just one or two others—in vulnerability and love, God shows up.

There is healing in being seen. There is restoration in being known. Even letting someone in just a little can become a turning point—a reminder that we are not alone, not beyond reach, and not unworthy of care.

You don't need a crowd. You just need a connection. Let someone walk with you. Let them remind you of your worth on those days you don't remember. Because healing is not just about what happens within you—it's about what happens *between* us. And sometimes, the presence of another is the clearest echo of God's presence there is.

### *The Shadows May Try to Visit, But They Don't Stay.*

Healing doesn't mean you'll never feel low again. It doesn't promise that every day will be light and easy. There may still be moments when the shadows press in—old thoughts whisper, energy wanes, or sorrow lingers longer than expected.

Here's what's different now: you know the way through. The shadows may still brush against you from time to time, but they no longer have permission to stay. They no longer hold your name in their grasp. You are not who you were when the darkness first found you—you are someone who has been shaped by light in unseen places.

You've changed. You carry a quiet strength now, born not of striving but of surrender. You carry the memory of every small victory, every faithful breath, every whispered prayer that kept you anchored when the winds raged. You've learned how to reach for grace instead of despair. How to slow down instead of spiraling. How to reach for grace when old anxieties arise. How to listen for the still, small voice instead of those loud accusations of fear. You've learned how to steady your soul when the winds of uncertainty blow. You carry a deeper breath, a steadier heart, a memory etched into your bones that says, I have been here before, and I know the way home.

This is what healing has done: it has taught you that even when the atmosphere shifts, you do not have to shift with it. You have learned how to stand—not by your own strength, but by the One who steadies you. And when the night tries to fall again, you carry the secret it cannot steal: the light is no longer outside you. It lives within you now.

You're not starting over. You're returning—returning to tools, to rhythms, to the memory of who you are and who God has always been. If the shadows return, remember:

- You have breath
- You have practices that root you
- You have people who care
- And most of all, you have God's presence, still faithful, still near

This is what makes your path a *path of no return*. Not because you'll never struggle again—but because you will never again be untouched by what you've learned. Never again unaware of your worth. Never again believing the darkness is all there is. *You have walked through the valley. You have heard God's whisper. You have become. And even when the shadows knock on the door, you know now that you don't have to let them settle in.* You've learned to open the window and let the light back in—His light. You have learned that He has never stopped reaching for you—and will never stop walking with you.

## MOMENTS OF REFLECTION

❖ What rhythms or practices help you stay grounded when life feels uncertain?

________________________________________

________________________________________

________________________________________

________________________________________

❖ In what ways have you changed since the beginning of your healing journey?

________________________________________

________________________________________

________________________________________

________________________________________

❖ Who are the people who remind you of your strength and your light?

________________________________________

________________________________________

________________________________________

________________________________________

❖ When the shadows return, what truths can you return to?

________________________________________

________________________________________

________________________________________

________________________________________

❖ How do you sense God inviting you to live—not just as someone who survived, but as someone who is becoming whole?

________________________________________

________________________________________

________________________________________

________________________________________

## CLOSING PRAYER

Dear God of light and lasting presence,
You have walked with me through darkness,
You have sat with me in silence,
and You have led me gently into places I never thought I'd find again –
places of peace, places of hope, and places of purpose.
Thank You for the healing that has begun,
for the courage that has grown,
and for the light that now resides in me.
Help me to remember that I am not alone,
not alone when the shadows visit,
not alone when the days feel long,
not alone even when I forget how far I've come.
Ground me in rhythms of grace.
Surround me with life-giving people.
Keep calling me back to Your presence,
again and again.
Let my life now be a witness –
not of perfection, but of Your restoration.
In Jesus' name I pray. Amen.

### AFFIRMATION

*I am no longer just surviving. I am becoming. The light has returned, and it lives in me. Even if the shadows visit, they do not get to stay. God is with me, and I will not go back.*

# CHAPTER 11

# Transformation and Renewed Vision: Life After Depression

There was a time in my life when hope felt like a stranger—or perhaps like a language I'd once known but could no longer speak. Everything felt dim, distant, and disconnected. But healing crept in the way dawn breaks—softly, slowly, with sacred stillness. And somewhere in the quiet, the light slowly returned. Not all at once. And definitely not with fanfare—rather, in soft moments and sacred pauses. But it returned, nonetheless.

With that light came a new vision—not just of the world around me, but of the life I was meant to live. A life no longer marked solely by survival, but by purpose. A life that had room for joy, presence, connection, and meaning.

This chapter is not a tidy ending. It isn't a ribbon tied neatly around the pain you've endured or a declaration that all is now perfect. Healing is rarely that linear—and rarely that clean. This is not the conclusion of your story. This is a *threshold.* A holy pause. A sacred turning point.

If you have applied the principles contained in this book to your life, you stand now on the edge of something new. Not untouched by the valley, but transformed by it. You've walked through the wilderness. You've sat in the shadows. You've cried until your soul ached, wrestled with silence, breathed prayers you weren't sure were even heard. You've rested. You've risen. You've kept going. And though not every scar has faded, and not every question has been answered, you are no longer who you were when the journey began.

Depression is part of your story—but it is not the whole of it. It may have shaped your perspective, slowed your steps, and redefined your path. But it does not define your worth. It does not get the last word. You are not broken beyond repair. You are beloved beyond measure. You are not just healing—you are being redeemed. Day by day, moment by moment, the broken places are being restored into something more whole, more beautiful, and more deeply rooted in grace. Despair is behind you—it is not the final word.

***The final word is life.***

This is your invitation to step forward—not perfectly, not fearlessly, but *faithfully.* You don't have to have everything figured out. You don't need to feel fully ready. But you can begin.

You've been through a valley, yes. But you've also grown roots. You've learned how to sit in stillness, how to listen in the silence, how to breathe through sorrow, and how to let grace find you in the dark. That wisdom—hard-won and holy—goes with you now.

This next season isn't about proving that you're better. It's about living from what's been made new. About honoring the story that shaped you, while no longer being confined by it. You are not simply someone who "got through it." You are someone who has become.

You've become more compassionate. More attuned to the sacred. More courageous in your tenderness. And now, you carry something within you that wasn't there before—an inner knowing, a deeper resilience, a quiet strength. These are gifts you didn't ask for, but they've been forged in you all the same.

So walk forward. Not to leave the past behind, but to live more fully in light of what you've learned. Step into your relationships, your purpose, your ordinary days, with a heart that knows healing is not a one-time event—it's a way of being. You are still becoming, yes. But you're not waiting to become whole—you're already walking in it. Every step you take, every truth you embrace, every moment you choose to stay open to God's presence is part of the wholeness unfolding in you.

This is indeed a new beginning. A sacred threshold. The shadows no longer get the final say. The Light does. And the Light is calling you forward into new life.

***You are not who you were.***

Healing has a way of changing us in ways we don't always notice right away. It doesn't announce itself with grand declarations. It reveals itself in the subtle shifts—the way you speak more gently to yourself, the way you extend grace to others, the way your heart softens in the presence of someone else's pain.

You may not have seen it happening. You may still feel fragile or unfinished. But take a closer look. The old urgency to prove yourself has quieted. The inner critic that once demanded perfection now meets resistance. You're learning to pause instead of push. To rest instead of perform. To sit with yourself without running.

These are the signs of transformation. Not perfection, but presence. Not certainty, but compassion. You are more attuned to what truly matters. You recognize the sacred in stillness. You listen more deeply—to your spirit, to others, to God. What once broke you open has now become the soil where new life has taken root.

This is what healing gives us: not a return to who we used to be, but a revelation of who we are becoming. You carry wisdom now that only suffering could cultivate. You carry resilience that wasn't born of striving, but surrender. You are no longer defined by what happened *to you*—but by what God is doing *in you*.

You are not who you were. You are someone new—softened by grace, strengthened by truth, and made whole by Love.

***Embrace becoming who you were meant to be.***

Life after depression isn't perfect. There are still days that require tenderness. Still moments that call for quiet strength. But something fundamental has changed—you are no longer trying to find your way back. You are moving forward into someone new. Someone *truer*. Someone more fully alive.

Healing has given you more than relief from suffering. It has given you perspective. Depth. Discernment. It has revealed parts of yourself you never had the space, or permission, to explore before. Now, as the light returns, you see life differently. You move with more intention. You speak with more honesty. You rest with more trust.

This is not about reinventing yourself. It's about true self-discovery—coming home to who you've always been beneath the layers of fear, expectation, and pain. Depression may have dimmed your vision for a season, clouding the truth of your worth and your identity. But healing, slow and sacred, has helped to clear the fog. It has reawakened your ability to see clearly again—not just the world around you, but the beauty within you. Now, you're beginning to see what truly matters: the gift of presence, the power of connection, the quiet grace of beauty, the anchoring of meaning, and the unwavering compass of truth. You're not creating a new version of yourself—you're reclaiming the truest version, the one that was never lost to God, even when you felt lost to yourself.

Maybe your truest self is revealed in the way you linger over coffee with a friend, in the quiet joy of creativity, in the soft light of morning prayer, in the sacredness of your work, or in small, unnoticed acts of compassion. Maybe it's in the gentleness you now offer yourself, or in the boundaries you've learned to honor. Perhaps it looks like releasing what once drained you—old expectations, unhealthy rhythms, silent self-criticism—so you can make space for what brings life: rest, purpose, grace, delight.

This vision isn't random or manufactured. It's sacred. It's the fruit of your journey through the valley, the slow harvest of every tear, every prayer, every choice to keep going when you felt like giving up. It has been planted in darkness and tended with faith.

And now, it is beginning to bloom. So embrace it—not with pressure or perfectionism, but with holy curiosity. Let your renewed purpose unfold naturally, like light breaking at the edge of a long night. There's no need to force clarity. You don't have to have every answer. Becoming isn't a goal to be achieved—it's a life to be lived. And you are already living it.

What lies ahead is not a demand—it's an invitation. An invitation to live honestly, rooted in what matters most. To live slowly, with space for your soul to breathe. To live joyfully, receiving goodness as a gift rather than earning it. To live as the person God has been gently shaping all along—not in spite of your journey, but because of it.

***Your story has power.***

You may not have chosen the path you've walked, but every step has shaped you. And whether you realize it yet or not, your story holds power—sacred, quiet, life-giving power.

The journey through depression is not just something you endured; it is something God has redeemed. Even if your story never makes its way into a public platform or a published page, it carries weight. It matters—because *you* matter. Your transformation is your testimony. You are living proof that healing is possible. That light returns. That silence breaks. That faith can survive the storm. And not just survive—but deepen. You are evidence that God still restores souls, still lifts the lowly, still brings beauty from ashes.

Maybe you will share your journey aloud someday—with a friend, a support group, a congregation, or an audience you never imagined. Maybe your words will help someone else feel less alone. But even if your story stays tucked inside the pages of your journal or the corners of your prayers, it has already done sacred work.

Because your story is not only about what you've come through—it's about *who you've become through it.* It has made you more grounded. More compassionate. More attuned to the presence of God in unexpected places.

And if the time comes to speak it—do so not out of pressure, but out of freedom. Speak from a place of grace. Because your voice might be the lifeline someone else is waiting for.

Even now, your story is echoing beyond what you can

see. It carries hope—not because it's flawless, but because it's real. Hope is not a distant promise. It is the companion that walks with you. It carries truth—not polished and perfect, but lived and embodied. It carries light—the kind that doesn't deny the dark but shines more beautifully because of it.

In addition, your story is not small. It is sacred. Every page, even the ones marked with pain, is being woven into something redemptive. And as you continue to walk forward—not as someone who has it all figured out, but as someone who is still becoming—you carry the invitation for others to do the same.

### *Your story Is still unfolding, and hope goes with you.*

If you're still somewhere in the middle—still waiting for the light to return fully, still learning to trust your own voice again—please know this: *you are not behind.* Healing is not a race, and your pace is not a problem. There is no clock counting down your worth, no deadline for restoration. You are not falling short because you're still healing—you're simply on the sacred timeline of becoming.

There is no finish line you have to reach in order to be worthy of peace or joy. These aren't rewards for having everything figured out. They're gifts of grace—freely given, even in the middle of the mess. You don't have to "arrive" somewhere to be allowed to breathe deeply, laugh again, or rest. You are allowed to receive joy now. You are allowed to taste peace, even as your healing continues. Wholeness is not a future destination—it's something God begins cultivating in you right here, in the unfolding.

Healing is not a straight path, and transformation is not a one-time event. It's a sacred unfolding—layer by layer, moment by moment. Some days you will feel strong. Other days you will need to rest. Both are part of the journey. Both are holy.

And if you have tasted renewal, if laughter has returned, if purpose is taking shape, if your heart beats with gratitude again, celebrate it. Not as the end of your healing, but as the beginning of something new. A new way of living. A new way of seeing. A new way of loving others and yourself.

You are walking forward now—not as someone untouched by suffering, but as someone *transformed* by grace. There will still be unknowns. There will still be quiet questions. But now you carry tools, truth, and testimony. Now you know where to turn when the shadows whisper. Now you recognize the voice of the One who never left your side.

Let your story continue to speak. In the hands of a faithful God, your story helps others find their way home. So let it deepen and grow. Let your light shine. Let it become even more beautiful than you imagined. And as it continues to unfold, remember that you are still becoming. And hope goes with you.

## MOMENTS OF REFLECTION

- ❖ In what ways has your perspective shifted since beginning your healing journey?

_______________________________________________

_______________________________________________

_______________________________________________

_______________________________________________

- ❖ What are some specific signs of healing or transformation that you now recognize in your life? Are there parts that you are beginning to see with more compassion or clarity?

_______________________________________________

_______________________________________________

_______________________________________________

_______________________________________________

- ❖ What does it mean to you to live with a renewed vision?

_______________________________________________

_______________________________________________

_______________________________________________

_______________________________________________

- ❖ How might you carry what you've learned into your relationships, your purpose, and your everyday moments?

____________________

____________________

____________________

____________________

- ❖ How do you want to carry hope into the next season of your life?

____________________

____________________

____________________

____________________

## CLOSING PRAYER

Dear God of restoration and new beginnings,
Thank You for walking with me through every shadowed valley
and never letting me go.
Thank You for the healing that came in whispers and a still small voice.
Thank You for the hope that returned like the dawn.
Thank You for the purpose that slowly took root within me.
I give to You my past—not wanting to hide it, but to honor it.

I give to You my present—not with a desire to control it, but to live it fully.
And I give to You my future—not with a spirit of fear, but with open hands.
Let my life reflect Your grace.
Let my story, whether spoken or silent,
be a light to someone still searching for theirs.
Even when I falter, remind me of how far I've come.
Even when I forget, remind me of who I am and of whose I am:
I am Yours. Loved. Whole. Becoming.
I trust that the story is still unfolding –
and that You go with me every step of the way.
In Jesus' name I pray. Amen.

### FINAL AFFIRMATION

*I am no longer defined by my darkest moments. I am living in the light of grace. My healing is real. My story is still unfolding. And hope goes with me—wherever I go.*

## EPILOGUE

# An Invitation to Keep Becoming

If you've come to this final page, whether you journeyed slowly through each chapter or read through more quickly, I want to thank you—for showing up. For being curious. For being open. Whether you journaled through the reflection prompts or simply read with quiet consideration, you've allowed something sacred to stir.

Maybe you've walked your own valley of depression and felt understood for the first time. Or maybe you're still on the edge of your healing, unsure where to begin. Either way, this book is not a test of progress. It's an offering. A path. A companion.

And now, you're invited to keep walking. If you haven't yet paused to reflect, to write, to bring your story to God through the exercises offered—know that it's not too late. Healing doesn't expire. Reflection doesn't have a deadline.

This book is here for you whenever you're ready to return to it—not to start over, but to go deeper.

Let this be your gentle encouragement: Do the work, not as a burden, but as a kindness to your soul. Give yourself space to name your pain, to explore your story, and to listen for what healing wants to say. You don't need to have all the answers. You only need to begin.

And if you have walked the road alongside these pages—if you've cried, remembered, released, or rejoiced—know that the work you've done is holy. Quiet. Sacred. Nothing is wasted. Every moment of reflection, every prayer, every brave step toward truth has made room for transformation.

There's more to your story, and it's still unfolding. Healing isn't a finish line—it's a way of living. A way of becoming.

And as you go forward, may this truth stay with you:

> *"Healing begins the moment we tell the truth about our pain and choose to stay with it long enough to discover that God's love has been waiting there all along."*
>
> —Swanzi Saunders-Davis

www.ingramcontent.com/pod-product-compliance
Lightning Source LLC
Chambersburg PA
CBHW070043100426
42740CB00013B/2783